Biblical Games

Biblical Games: A Strategic Analysis of Stories in the Old Testament

Steven J. Brams

The MIT Press
Cambridge, Massachusetts, and
London, England

This book was set in VIP Palatino by DEKR
Corporation and printed and bound by
The Murray Printing Company in the
United States of America.

Library of Congress Cataloging in
Publication Data
Brams, Steven J
Biblical games.

Includes bibliographical references and
index.
1. Bible. O.T.—Criticism, interpretation,
etc.
2. Game theory. I. Title.
BS1171.2.B7   221.6   80-10529
ISBN 0-262-02144-7

To the memory of
Oskar Morgenstern
1902–1977

Contents

5   *Protracted Conflict*

6   *Just Agreements and Wise Arbitration*

7   *Royal Conflict*

8 *Conflict Between the Sexes*

9 *Theory, Evidence, and Findings*

Notes

General Index

Index of Biblical Passages

List of Figures

Preface

The inspiration for this book came from teaching an undergraduate humanities seminar called "Biblical Games" at New York University in the spring of 1978. Humanities seminars at NYU have received support from the Mellon Foundation, to which I am grateful. I am also grateful to the students in the seminar for incisive ideas and trenchant criticisms.

I recognize that my approach to the study and understanding of the Old Testament will be controversial. I have, however, tried to avoid being deliberately provocative. Having approached the Bible with what I consider a reasonably open mind, I believe the interpretations offered and conclusions reached are founded pretty much on the biblical text.

No one, of course, reads anything with a completely untutored mind. In my case, the "strategic analysis" in the subtitle of this book is informed by game theory and decision theory, about which I will have more to say in the first chapter.

Having done this analysis, I am more convinced than ever that a modern scientific theory can be applied to classic humanistic material. Not only can it illuminate this material with a breadth and depth that less systematic and rigorous approaches cannot but the theory also can be applied by other researchers. This permits alternative interpretations to be checked for plausibility and consistency and facilitates comparisons among them.

Instead of making a god of science or belaboring my approach, however, I prefer to let the reader judge what fruits strategic theory, applied to the Old Testament, bears. For convenience I shall henceforth use only the masculine pronoun form in this book—except when specifically referring to women—but that should not be read as any slight on women, who figure very prominently in many biblical games.

Several people read parts or the entire manuscript and contributed greatly to my enlightenment about a number of matters. For their valuable comments and criticisms, I am grateful to James P. Carse, Baruch A. Levine, Douglas Muzzio, William H. Riker, Philip D. Straffin Jr., and Rabbi Dov Taylor, all of whom should be absolved of blame for the deficiencies that remain in the book. I am also indebted to Nancy Fernandez, who accurately typed the manuscript and made several useful suggestions.

Most of all, I thank my wife Eva for balancing an abiding faith in the project with a profound and detailed critique of the manuscript. I cannot accuse our children, Julie and Michael, of great devotion to the project, but I would not disparage their rationality.

Biblical Games

The dogmas of the quiet past are inadequate for the stormy present.

Abraham Lincoln

One understands nothing of the works of God unless he starts from the principle that God willed to blind some and enlighten others.

Blaise Pascal
Pensées

The description of God as a Person is indispensable for everyone who like myself means by "God" not a principle . . . not an idea . . . but who rather means by "God," as I do, him who—whatever else he may be—enters into a direct relation with us. . . .

Martin Buber
I and Thou, Postscript

Mathematics is no more than symbolism. But it is the only symbolism invented by the human mind which steadfastly resists the constant attempts of the mind to shift and smudge the meaning. It is the only exact symbolism and, by being exact, it is self-correcting.

J. Bronowski and Bruce Mazlish
The Western Intellectual Tradition

Introduction

The Bible is a sacred document to millions of people. It expresses supernatural elements of faith that do not admit of any natural explanations. At the same time, however, some of the great narratives in the Bible do not seem implausible reconstructions of events. Indeed, biblical characters exhibit on occasion common human failings in their behavior toward one another.

Is it possible to reconcile natural and supernatural elements in the Bible? This would not seem an easy task for God, in some ineffable manifestation, makes His presence felt in practically all biblical stories. A naturalistic interpretation of the Bible immediately confronts His commanding presence and uniqueness.

In any biblical analysis or interpretation, then, God must be given His proper due. He *is* the central character in the Bible. Accordingly, I propose to treat Him as such, but my treatment assumes more than His omnipresence. I also assume that God is motivated to do certain things—that He has goals He would like to achieve.

I do not assume that God is omnipotent. To be sure, He can perform miracles and even endow others with great powers. But the Bible is clear on one thing: human beings *do* have free will and can exercise it, even if it invokes God's wrath. (Reasons why God chose not to make man a puppet are given in chapter 2.) Consequently, God, powerful as He is, is sometimes thwarted in His desires.

Since God does not always get His way, He can properly be viewed as a participant, or *player*, in a game. This is so because a *game*—as the term is used in game theory—is an interdependent decision situation whose outcome depends on the choices of *all* players.

When God is frustrated by His inability to dictate the outcome because His desires are deflected by other players' choices, the Bible tells us that He may be angry, jealous, or vengeful—and His actions tend to reflect these emotions. Seen in this light, God is a very human character, despite His unique presence and awe-inspiring powers. This is not, of course, the way most religions view God. Indeed, the Bible continually portrays Him as not only awesome but unknowable, as utterly beyond our comprehension. The clear implication is that He is incapable of being calculating and conniving, of stooping to the level of "playing games."

Yet this is not the impression that many of God's actions convey. In fact, since God Himself often provides explicit reasons for acting in a particular way, it is hard to maintain that His motivations and design are unfathomable.

Is it not sensible, then, to imagine

God as a game player who chooses among different courses of action to try to achieve certain goals? Similarly, is it not reasonable that more ordinary characters in the Bible, knowing of God's presence, make choices to further their own ends in light of possible consequences they perceive can occur?

Although the idea that God and a cast of human characters play games may seem bizarre if not preposterous, I shall try to show in a variety of biblical stories that this is not only a reasonable interpretation but also that the players in these games—including God—acted rationally. That is, given their preferences and their knowledge of other players' preferences, they made strategy choices that would lead to better rather than worse outcomes. A more precise definition of rationality will be given later.

With the publication of *Theory of Games and Economic Behavior* in 1944,[1] the mathematical theory of games was born and has since been the stimulus for scores of books and thousands of articles on game theory and its applications. Rarely, however, has game theory been applied to humanistic material; its principal applications have been to the social sciences, mainly economics and political science. To the best of my knowledge, there has not previously been a book-length treatment of a humanistic or literary work that makes serious use of game theory.[2]

It is true, of course, that the language of "games" and "play" has often been loosely invoked in studies of the Bible. But the insights of such treatments have been just that—insights in search of a theory. For reasons I shall indicate later in this chapter, good ideas or insights, while necessary, are not sufficient for bringing coherence to a work as complex and profound as the Bible.

I wish to stress at the outset that I make no claim that every story in the Old Testament can be cast in a game-theoretic framework. (I would make a similar disclaimer for the New Testament, but that is a sufficiently different body of work that I would withhold any comparisons pending further study.)[3] Most amenable to this approach are biblical stories that involve significant conflict and intrigue, wherein characters can plausibly be assumed to think about the consequences of alternative actions they might take before choosing them. Indeed, many of these stories are part of the so-called wisdom literature of the Bible precisely because they serve the didactic purpose of trumpeting the (God-inspired) virtues of cleverness and sagacity in ticklish or harrowing situations.

Contrary to the popular notion of a game, choices in game theory are not assumed to be frivolous. Quite the contrary: players in games are assumed to think carefully about their choices and the possible choices of other players. Whether the outcome of a game is comic or tragic, fun or serious, fair or unfair, it depends on individual *choices.*

I italicize "choices" since I wish to use game theory to explain the decisions made and actions taken in specific situations, based on the preferences of the players. Thus, preferences are used to explain choices; if preferences are not entirely clear, I consider alternative rankings and determine what consequences they have for the making of rational choices. As will become evident, this search may lead to significant alternative explanations of biblical choices.

But is still another exegesis of the Bible needed, especially one that carries the baggage of a mathematical theory that is not always easy to understand? If the import of this question is that an arcane theory lifted from one domain and applied to another may simply be inappropriate, I emphatically agree. Deep insight is certainly better than a rigorous theory dryly and unimaginatively applied. In biblical scholarship, as in everything else, there is no substitute for illuminating ideas, familiarity with the subject matter, and good intuition. Admirable as these qualities are, however, they may not be sufficient when the complexity of the material is overwhelming. If the amount written about the Bible is an index of its complexity, then the Bible is indeed awesomely complex.

Game theory, in my opinion, is a tool ideally suited for penetrating the complex decision-making situations often described in the Bible.[4] Because its application requires the careful unraveling of a tangle of character motivations and their effects, it imposes a discipline on the study of these situations that is usually lacking in more traditional literary-historical-theological analyses of the Bible. These analyses often suffer, in my opinion, from their unrestrained arbitrariness in finding linkages, seeing parallels, and generally trying to tie things together—somehow—with valiant leaps of imagination. An assemblage of random insights, unconnected by any logically structured view of the world that might be called a framework or theory, does not provide a parsimonious or compelling intellectual organization of the Bible. Understanding requires organization, and organization is given by a theory.

A word about the parts of game theory I have utilized in this book is perhaps in order. I have relied almost exclusively upon what is called the "noncooperative" theory,

making use of both the "extensive" (game tree) and "normal" (matrix) forms of games in the analysis. Also, I have assumed only ordinal preferences (players can rank, but not attach numerical values to, outcomes) and no probabilistic calculations, except, on one occasion, to indicate "chance" as a player with unspecified probabilities.

I have eschewed cooperative game theory, cardinal utilities, and expected-value calculations because I think the Bible provides insufficient information to support applications of these concepts. As Erich Auerbach observed, the Bible is spare in the details it offers of the thoughts and feelings of characters; stories often unroll with motives and purposes unexpressed. While the "foreground" is bare, however, the "background" is deep and multilayered, making possible inferences about characters whose situations echo a past "fraught with background."[5] Although Auerbach considers—unjustifiably, in my opinion—a rationalistic interpretation of the Bible to be "psychologically absurd,"[6] he also says that the daily life of the characters is "permeated with the stuff of conflict,"[7] which I consider exactly the raw data to which game theory is uniquely applicable.

If the more esoteric and mathematically deeper aspects of game theory offer little to elucidate this conflict, it is fair to ask whether the elementary, nonquantitative theory has the power and depth to cast new and penetrating light on an old subject. In my opinion it does, but probably more in the sense of providing the unified theoretical perspective I spoke of earlier than making intricate and subtle connections. To supplement this austere perspective, I have frequently resorted to a verbal explication of a strategic situation that uses ideas from game theory but not its formal tools when a rote application of the theory seemed silly or forced. Game theory is certainly not a deus ex machina, especially in the context of a work that already has one God!

In the biblical narratives to be analyzed, I shall first summarize the relevant story and then attempt to model it, by which I mean construct a simplified representation of the strategic situation which nonetheless captures its essential features. When new technical concepts are first introduced in the book, I shall define and explain them in the concrete context of the story being modeled. This, I believe, will make them more real and impart to the reader unfamiliar with these concepts a better intuitive understanding of their meaning and significance.

With the exception of the Adam and Eve story covered in chapter 2,

the chapters are developed around particular themes. Within each chapter, I usually proceed chronologically, starting with stories in earlier books or sections of the Old Testament and proceeding to stories in later books or sections. I have been highly selective in my choice of stories, generally concentrating on well-known narratives found in the earlier books. This eclectic choice is in part dictated by the fact that many of the most interesting and significant conflicts occur in the first part of the Old Testament, and in part because I thought I could best illustrate the utility of the game-theoretic analysis if many of the stories were already familiar, thereby facilitating comparisons with traditional interpretations.

I have quoted extensively from the Bible throughout this book to give the reader some flavor of its direct, vivid, and dramatic language. All passages are taken from recent translations by the Jewish Publication Society of America, which I consider the most accurate modern English translations of the Old Testament.[8]

Let me offer some advice on reading this book for those unfamiliar with game theory. Most of the basic concepts are defined and illustrated in chapter 2. I strongly recommend studying these carefully through the examples in this chapter. Once these are understood, I believe the rest of the book can be read quite painlessly. Nevertheless, I realize that payoff matrices and game trees do not reveal themselves at a glance, so I have tried in the figures to make their secrets as accessible as possible through the use of descriptive aids. Since the Bible itself is not exactly light reading, it is perhaps unreasonable to expect that any attempt at an exegesis of some of its difficult ideas is going to be a paragon of simplicity. To understand a profound document requires a seriousness of purpose, but certainly one point of this book is that one does not have to be overly sanctimonious about one's approach to studying the Bible.

My analysis of biblical games and my rational explications of the choices of their players will in some cases be controversial. Where the reader disagrees with assumptions I have made about who the players in a game are, what strategy choices were available to them, the outcomes that they saw as possible, or their preferences for these outcomes, I urge him to experiment with different assumptions. The game-theoretic framework, in my opinion, should not be rejected out of hand simply because there are alternative—if not superior—strategic representations of the situations that I have presented.

Equally controversial, if not shocking, may be the philosophical,

religious, and theological implications I have drawn from the analysis. I have not shunned these, because I believe that the ultimate significance of this analysis rests on the ramifications it has for the meaning of God and His relationship to the human world He created. (These questions are discussed in the final chapter, which some readers may want to skip to immediately to see where the strategic analysis leads before pursuing it in depth.) Since God's place in the scheme of things helps to define man's and woman's as well, I believe the games I have analyzed also have something edifying to say about human experience and its spiritual connection.

This connection is defined by the games God and human characters play. Only a detailed and searching study of the particular strategies players chose and the outcomes they obtained, however, provides one with a touchstone for comparing, and understanding the significance of, one's own choices and experiences in life. This is certainly one of the benefits of looking again at the Bible.

2   The Creation and Its Aftermath

2.1 Introduction

Everyone knows the story of Adam and Eve. Their temptation by the serpent and their subsequent banishment from the garden of Eden seem a simple enough tale which hardly calls for extended game-theoretic analysis. Why, then, devote a whole chapter to games played at the creation and just afterward?

I will respond in three ways. First, since what happened at and immediately following the creation sets the stage for all future events in the Bible, it does not seem unreasonable to undertake a close analysis of the motivations and actions of the principal players—including God—at the beginning. Moreover, more than any other portion of the Old Testament, it is the creation that challenges the whole raison d'être of this work: naturalistic, not to say rationalistic, explanations of the creation and the beginning of history have been highly controversial. Thus, if the actions of the players at the beginning can be rationally explicated in a satisfactory way, the stage is better set for a consistent and unified analysis of other stories. On the other hand, if what started it all is awkwardly ignored, this omission would be, at best, embarrassing; at worst, it would cast doubt on the utility of the whole enterprise.

Second, the analysis of the creation provides a perspective from which to view the actions and motivations of players in ensuing biblical games. This perspective is important, because the actions some players, particularly God, deem necessary seem to shift while the external circumstances remain the same. Does this apparent inconsistency indicate irrational behavior, or is it rational in light of new goals or preferences? In general, I take the latter view and will try to show how it is supported in specific instances.

A third reason for starting the analysis at the creation is to show that the creation and its aftermath was a much more complex decision-making situation than is sometimes assumed. Several interrelated decisions were made by the different casts of characters. Yet, when these decisions are delinated as sequential choices in a set of games, I believe this complexity can be rendered perspicuous.

Mountains of material have been written about the creation and the story of Adam and Eve. Almost none of it, however, including a very extensive archeological literature, is relevant to the problems of choice faced by these biblical characters at the beginning of history. In this chapter I shall try to show that Adam and Eve's choices, the serpent's, and God's formed links in a logical chain that game theory helps one to forge.

2.2 The Creation of the World

Chapter 1 of Genesis describes how the world was created in six days. Starting with a world "unformed and void" (Gen. 1:2),

God said, "Let there be light"; and there was light. God saw that the light was good, and God separated the light from the darkness. (Gen. 1:3–4)

No reason is given why God undertook to make heaven and earth; that the initial result (light) pleased Him, however, is clear: He "saw that the light was good."

At subsequent stages in the creation, after observing the products of His efforts, God repeated that "this was good" (Gen. 1:10, 12, 18, 21, 25); indeed, after creating man and woman and other living creatures on the sixth day, God "found it very good" (Gen. 1:31). Obviously pleased with Himself, God ceased His work on the seventh day, blessing this day and declaring it holy.[1]

Not only did God stop working on the seventh day, but the Bible also reports that He "ceased from all the work of creation which He had done" (Gen. 2:3). Thus, God appears to have had a set number of tasks, each of which He evaluated before going on to a new task. Since all appeared to be going well at each stage, God was motivated to continue until He was finished.

This sounds like a sensible strategy: break up a big job into smaller tasks; after completing each, evaluate the results; if the evaluations are favorable, continue; if not, stop. Of course, it is impossible to say in the hypothetical case of unfavorable evaluations how bad the results would have had to have been for God to have decided to cut His losses (reckoned, presumably, in time and wasted effort). But since this was not the case, I conclude that God was a rational planner who followed an incremental strategy that did not entail undue risk.

To say that God was rational in the sense of avoiding unnecessary risk, and possibly big losses if things turned sour, does not answer the question of why He undertook the job of creating the world in the first place. It is one thing to plan a job carefully; it is quite another to decide that the job is even worth doing. Although the Bible says simply that God acted, without giving a reason why, Leszek Kolakowski thinks the reason is transparent:

God created the world for His own glory. This is an indisputable fact and

one, moreover, that is quite understandable. A greatness that nobody can see is bound to feel ill at ease. Actually, under such circumstances one has no desire whatsoever to be great. Greatness would be pointless, it would serve no purpose. . . . Holiness and greatness are possible only in a concrete setting. . . . And only then [after the creation of the world] did He really become great, for now He had someone who could admire Him and to whom He could compare Himself—and how favorably![2]

2.3 The Question of Free Will

Was it only loneliness, and the need to be admired, that drove God to create the world? There is no hint of this in the biblical statement that there was "no man to till the soil" (Gen. 2:5). Presumably, God did not have to create man "in His image" (Gen. 1:27) to accomplish such a mundane agricultural task.

God obviously had better things in mind for man and woman when He directed them to

be fertile and increase, fill the earth and master it; and rule the fish of the sea, the birds of the sky, and all the living things that creep on earth. (Gen. 1:28)

If this were not enough,

the LORD God planted a garden in Eden, in the east, and placed there the man whom He had formed. And from the ground the LORD God caused to grow every tree that was pleasing to the sight and good for food, with the tree of life in the middle of the garden, and the tree of knowledge of good and bad. (Gen. 2:8-9)

Yet the garden of Eden was not quite idyllic, nor its human inhabitants quite so pure of heart, that conflict could not arise. In fact, God set the stage for a challenge to His authority when He commanded man:

Of every tree of the garden you are free to eat; but as for the tree of knowledge of good and bad, you must not eat of it; for as soon as you eat of it, you shall die. (Gen. 2:16-17)

This admonition would hardly be necessary if man (and later woman) were simply God's puppets, blindly attentive to His every wish and command.

As I have already shown, God was a careful planner, so it seems unlikely that He would have created a man with free will whom He could not control if this were not His intention. Thus, in creating the world, I assume God most preferred to create man with free will; failing that, I presume man as a puppet would be better than no man at all. After all, if God truly

craved admiration, as Kolakowski maintains, it would be better to be admired by a superior person created in one's own image than ordinary animals.

Worse, I suppose, would be not to create man at all and have only the plants and animals to behold. Moreover, without man, there would be nobody to rule over other living creatures. Still worse would be to remain a solitary God without even a world to look down upon, much less anyone to proclaim one's glory. In summary, I assume God's ranking of alternatives from best to worst was the following:

1. Create man with free will.
2. Create man as a puppet.
3. Create world without man.
4. Create no world.

By choosing His most-preferred alternative, God acted rationally.

God's preference for man with free will over man as a puppet perhaps requires further justification, especially in light of the grief and anguish that man later caused God. (If God were omniscient, could not this be anticipated?) To begin with, I believe that as much as God sought glory and desired praise, He recognized that it would be empty if man were but His puppet. God wanted man to pay Him homage, but homage that was heartfelt, not forced or dictated. As Elie Wiese' put it, "God loves man to be clear-sighted and outspoken, not blindly obsequious."[3] This view is supported by evidence presented in later chapters that God most relished unswerving faith when man was in his direst straits. In such circumstances, a man, not a puppet, can be tested.

God relentlessly tests man throughout the Bible, giving him multiple opportunities to sin. The results are mixed: sometimes man succeeds impressively; sometimes he fails miserably; and sometimes he falters before regaining his faith. If man were an unalloyed success in all these tests, then the world would be a dull place—precisely, it seems, what God wanted to escape from in creating the world in the first place.

To make the world less predictable and therefore more alive and engrossing, it was in God's interest to give man free will. The price He paid, of course, is having to contend with a creature who continually frustrates Him and occasionally drives Him to the brink of despair. But when man succeeds, God can not only feel proud but also rest assured that man's profession of faith is genuine and not mere flattery, which presumably makes man's character defects worth tolerating.

Not surprisingly, God is selective in what kinds of men and women He supports. As befits a demanding creator, He continually makes judgments about the deeds and misdeeds of His subjects. Having made up His mind, He is not above playing favorites, as I shall show in many later stories.

2.4 The Imposition of Constraints

To decide whom to help and support, it would appear rational for God to impose constraints on human activities. As noted in section 2.3, the first constraint God imposed on man was not to eat from the tree of knowledge of good and bad in the garden of Eden.

To demonstrate the value of constraints—on, surprisingly, man as well as God—consider the outcome matrix in figure 2.1. God, depicted as the row player, has two strategies in this two-person game:

1. Impose constraints: I.
2. Don't impose constraints: Ī.

Although I shall later distinguish games played separately by Adam and Eve, it is convenient to lump them together as a collective human player in the present analysis. (A *player* is simply an actor or actors who can make strategy choices in a *game*, which is defined in figure 2.1 by the strategies of the players and the outcomes to which they lead.)

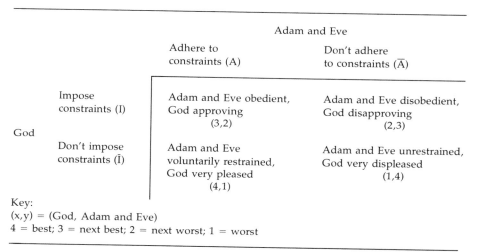

		Adam and Eve	
		Adhere to constraints (A)	Don't adhere to constraints ($\overline{A}$)
God	Impose constraints (I)	Adam and Eve obedient, God approving (3,2)	Adam and Eve disobedient, God disapproving (2,3)
	Don't impose constraints ($\overline{I}$)	Adam and Eve voluntarily restrained, God very pleased (4,1)	Adam and Eve unrestrained, God very displeased (1,4)

Key:
(x,y) = (God, Adam and Eve)
4 = best; 3 = next best; 2 = next worst; 1 = worst

Figure 2.1 Outcome matrix for constraint game

Like God, Adam and Eve have two strategies:

1. Adhere to constraints: A.

2. Don't adhere to constraints: $\overline{A}$.

One might ask what it means for God *not* to impose constraints and then for Adam and Eve to adhere to the (nonexistent) constraints. In this situation I assume that Adam and Eve are aware of God's preferences (to be described shortly) as to what constraints they might voluntarily observe. Similarly, God knows Adam and Eve's preferences. A game in which each player knows the other player's (or players') preferences is called a *game of complete information*. Henceforth,

games presented in this book will be assumed to be games of complete information unless otherwise indicated.

The consequences arising from the strategy choices of both players are summarized verbally in the *outcome matrix* shown in figure 2.1. (The pairs of numbers associated with the different outcomes define the preferences of the players and will be explained momentarily.) In fact, however, Adam and Eve did not have the choice of just an unconditionally cooperative (A) or noncooperative ($\overline{A}$) response. Their moves occurred after God's, in full knowledge of the strategy choice (I or $\overline{I}$) that God made.

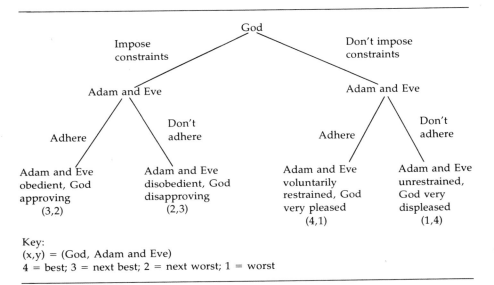

Key:
(x,y) = (God, Adam and Eve)
4 = best; 3 = next best; 2 = next worst; 1 = worst

Figure 2.2 Game tree for constraint game

The representation of this *sequence* of moves is shown by the game tree in figure 2.2 (read from top to bottom): God first chooses to impose or not impose constraints; only then do Adam and Eve choose to adhere or not adhere to these constraints. The fact that God's move precedes Adam and Eve's, and Adam and Eve are aware of God's prior choice, means that the game cannot properly be represented as a 2 × 2 game (two players, each with two strategy choices, assumed to be selected simultaneously), as illustrated by the outcome matrix in figure 2.1. Rather, the proper representation in matrix

form of the game between God, and Adam and Eve, is as a 2 × 4 game (God has two strategies, Adam and Eve have four), which I shall discuss presently.

For the purpose of evaluating the four possible outcomes that can occur, however, the 2 × 2 form will be used. It is a form that will be used in many later two-person games to explain the outcomes that can arise—independently of the sequence of moves—when the game tree is omitted.

In my evaluation, I attempt only to rank the outcomes for each player from best to worst, without attaching any specific values, or cardinal utilities, to these ranks. In the representation shown in figures 2.1 and 2.2, "4" is considered a player's best outcome; "3," next best; "2," next worst; and "1," worst. Hence, the higher the number, the better the outcome.

The first number, x, in each pair is assumed to be God's preference ranking (row player in figure 2.1); the second number, y, Adam and Eve's preference ranking (column player in figure 2.1). Thus, for example, the payoff (2,3) means the next-worst outcome for God, the next-best outcome for Adam and Eve.

Notice in this game that what is best (4) for one player is worst (1) for the other; and what is next best (3) for one player is next worst (2) for the other. Games like this in which the preferences of the players are diametrically opposed are called *games of total conflict* (or zero-sum games if cardinal utilities were assigned).

Now consider God's ranking of the four possible outcomes. I assume that God is very pleased (4) when He doesn't impose constraints and Adam and Eve are voluntarily restrained; approving (3) if they adhere to constraints he imposes; disapproving (2) when they don't adhere; and very displeased (1) when He imposes no constraints and they are unrestrained.

In the last case, presumably, God would rue the day He didn't impose constraints, because He cannot easily punish Adam and Eve retroactively for disobeying a nonexistent command. Although it may seem for God a more serious breach if Adam and Eve, by acting unrestrainedly, outrightly defied his prohibition, in my view God would prefer to be defied so He can exact later retribution without appearing to act arbitrarily. Hence, in figure 2.1, I rank $I\overline{A}$ better for God (2) than $\overline{I}\overline{A}$ (1).

As I already indicated, Adam and Eve's preferences are diametrically opposed to God's in this game. Their two best outcomes occur when they don't adhere to constraints; between these, they would obviously prefer not to defy God (when He doesn't impose constraints) than to defy Him (when He does). Their worst two outcomes occur when they adhere to God's constraints; voluntary compliance, I assume, is least attractive, because they could just as well have chosen not to comply without fear of retribution.

The assumption that Adam and Eve most prize their freedom from constraints requires further explanation. Would they really rather suffer God's wrath, and the possible punishment this brings, than accept certain limits on their activities? Surely, it might be argued, God's threat of death for eating from the tree of knowledge of good and bad should act as a sufficient deterrent.

Yet, consider how the serpent, "the shrewdest of all the wild beasts that the LORD God had made" (Gen. 3:1), effectively blunted this threat when it confronted Eve. First, it asked her, disingenuously,

Did God really say: You shall not eat of any tree of the garden? (Gen. 3:1)

Note that the serpent introduced into its question the information, which it presumably knew to be false, that there was (possibly) a prohibition against eating from *any* tree. When Eve responded that the fruit from only one tree "in the middle of the garden" (Gen. 3:3) was forbidden, the serpent made light of this prohibition:

You are not going to die, but God knows that as soon as you eat of it your eyes will be opened and you will be like divine beings [God] who know good and bad. (Gen. 3:4-5)

In fact, by acting naïvely in the beginning—not like the shrewd beast the reader is told it is—the serpent rendered itself more believable to Eve and was thereby better able to dispel her fears.

But more than laying to rest Eve's fears, the serpent also offered a good reason for eating the forbidden fruit: it would make her divine, or godlike. This reason was reinforced by the fact that "the tree was good for eating and a delight to the eyes, and . . . desirable as a source of wisdom" (Gen. 3:6).

Given these arguments (which I shall explore more fully in section 2.4), would it therefore not be sensible for Eve to defy God's constraint, and probably for Adam to do likewise? If so, what consequences does this preference for defiance (3) over compliance (2), given that God imposes constraints, have for rational play in the constraint game?

As noted earlier, the 2 × 2 game shown in figure 2.1 does not depict the constraint game that was actually played, though it *is* useful in depicting the four different outcomes that can arise and the preferences of the two players for each of them. Since God made the first strategy choice, as shown in the game tree of figure 2.2, the proper representation of this game for the purpose of determining better and worse strategies of the players is as a 2 × 4 game, in which God has two strategies and Adam and Eve have four.

The representation of the game is shown in figure 2.3. It reflects the fact that, since God has the first move, He can choose whether to impose or not impose constraints. Adam and Eve, on the other hand,

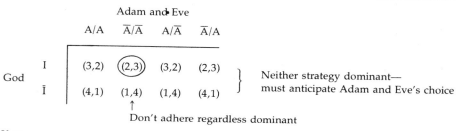

Key:
(x,y) = (God, Adam and Eve)
4 = best; 3 = next best; 2 = next worst; 1 = worst
Circled outcome rational

Figure 2.3 Payoff matrix for constraint game

whose moves occur only after God has made a choice, have four possible choices, depending on what God chooses. Thus, Adam and Eve have four *strategies*, or complete plans that describe their possible choices, contingent upon God's prior choices:

1. A/A *Adhere to constraints regardless:* Adhere if constraints imposed, adhere if not.

2. $\overline{A}/\overline{A}$ *Be unrestrained regardless:* Don't adhere if constraints imposed, don't adhere if not.

3. A/$\overline{A}$ *Tit-for-tat:* Adhere if constraints imposed, don't adhere if not.

4. $\overline{A}$/A *Tat-for-tit:* Don't adhere if constraints imposed, adhere if not.

Note that in A/A and $\overline{A}$/A, Adam and Eve would adhere to con-

straints that are not imposed. Given the assumption of complete information, I interpret this situation to mean that if God remained silent about constraints, Adam and Eve still recognized that He would most prefer (4) that they restrain themselves voluntarily, and similarly God knew that this would be anathema (1) for them. For Adam and Eve, however, it might be argued that their awareness of God's preferences for this and other outcomes did not materialize until *after* they had eaten from the tree of knowledge of good and bad and their eyes were thereby opened to the consequences of their defiance of God's prohibition.

Yet to accept this view means that God issued an empty threat, whose implications would not be understood by Adam and Eve. This seems to me implausible—God, for reasons already indicated, did not relish mindless adherence to His precepts. However, if it is believed that Adam and Eve did not know the consequences of their actions, I would maintain that God had at least in mind to teach the (now informed) descendants of Adam and Eve a lesson about defiance. But this is jumping ahead of the game that I believe in fact occurred.

The 2 × 4 payoff matrix in figure 2.3 gives the payoffs each player receives for every pair of strategy choices (two for God, four for Adam and Eve) of the two players. Thus, for example, if God chooses to impose constraints (I), and Adam and Eve chooses tat-for-tit ($\bar{A}/A$), I$\bar{A}$ is the resultant outcome, for the choice of I by God implies the choice of $\bar{A}$ by Adam and Eve under tat-for-tit. As can be seen from figure 2.1, this yields a payoff of (2,3)—the next-worst outcome for God, the next-best outcome for Adam and Eve—which is shown in the I row and $\bar{A}/A$ column of figure 2.3.

What are the game-theoretic implications of the preference assumptions I have made for God and for Adam and Eve? Notice, first, that Adam and Eve's strategy of being unrestrained regardless ($\bar{A}/\bar{A}$) is *dominant:* their payoffs associated with this strategy are at least as good as, and sometimes better

than, their payoffs associated with any of their other three strategies, whatever God chooses. Specifically, if God chooses I, $\bar{A}/\bar{A}$ yields Adam and Eve a payoff of 3, which is better than A/A and A/$\bar{A}$ yield (2) and as good as $\bar{A}/A$ yields; on the other hand, if God chooses $\bar{I}$, $\bar{A}/\bar{A}$ yields Adam and Eve a payoff of 4, which obviously cannot be improved upon. Thus, $\bar{A}/\bar{A}$ is Adam and Eve's *unconditionally* best strategy—not dependent on which strategy (I or $\bar{I}$) God chooses— and presumably the choice a rational player would make in this game. In fact, I define a *rational player* to be one who chooses a dominant strategy if he has one.[4]

Unlike Adam and Eve, God does not have an unconditionally best choice in the constraint game. If Adam and Eve should choose A/A or $\bar{A}/A$, God should choose $\bar{I}$, because this strategy would yield Him His best outcome of 4; however, if Adam and Eve should choose $\bar{A}/\bar{A}$ or A/$\bar{A}$, God should choose I, for this strategy would ensure him against obtaining his worst outcome (1) in both cases. The fact that neither I nor $\bar{I}$ is an unconditionally best choice for God—"best" depends on what Adam and Eve subsequently do—demonstrates that God does not have a dominant strategy in the constraint game.

What strategy, then, will God as a rational player choose? Since

Adam and Eve's strategy of $\overline{A}/\overline{A}$ (unrestrained regardless) is dominant, God would assume that as rational players they will choose it. Anticipating their choice of $\overline{A}/\overline{A}$, God will choose to impose constraints (I) because it yields Him a higher payoff (2) than does $\overline{I}$ (1). (In general, a player without a dominant strategy is *rational* if, for the dominant strategy choice of the other player, he chooses the strategy that yields him the highest-ranked outcome of those associated with the other player's dominant strategy.)

The choice of I by God, and $\overline{A}/\overline{A}$ by Adam and Eve, results in outcome (2,3). Since this is the outcome that would be chosen by rational players (defined earlier), I define it to be the *rational outcome*. Although it is the next-best outcome for Adam and Eve, it is only the next-worst outcome for God. Nevertheless, it is the product of rational play by both players and in fact was the outcome chosen in this biblical game.

It may seem strange that such a poor outcome for one player (especially God!) can be called "rational." As I shall show later, however, God partially recoups in the final punishment game He plays with Adam and Eve, realizing His next-best outcome. The constraint game and the two games that immediately follow (the temptation game and the sharing game) are preludes to this final game, which I think is the best gauge of God's—and the other players'—performance after the creation. As I shall show in subsequent sections, once Eve succumbed to the serpent's temptation, the serpent's success provided God with an excuse to display "evenhanded" justice—after extracting from Adam and Eve a confession of sin with an extenuating-circumstance plea.

Given the preferences of the players I have postulated, the analysis of this section demonstrates why it was in the interest of God to impose constraints on the behavior of Adam and Eve, and why it was in Eve's (and later Adam's) interest to ignore such constraints. However, the specific reasons why Eve succumbed to the inveiglements of the serpent—rather than just chose by her own lights to disobey God— can be better understood in the context of the game she played with the serpent, which, like other players, had preferences.

2.5 Eve's Temptation by the Serpent

I have already described the exchange that Eve and the serpent had. The serpent, it seems, wanted to engineer Eve's fall from divine favor, though its motives for desiring this are never made explicit. Being the shrewd beast that the Bible asserts it was, however, the serpent, I assume, knew full well the consequences of defying God and would have preferred not to tempt Eve if she would eat the forbidden fruit anyway. In fact, the question the serpent initially asked about what fruit God had forbidden Adam and Eve to eat was quite innocuous—ostensibly, the serpent only sought information.

As I suggested in section 2.4, however, this question seemed cleverly designed to elicit from Eve the statement that only one tree was off limits. The apparent implication of this question was that God's prohibition could not be serious if it applied to only one tree in the entire garden of Eden.

But, unfortunately for the serpent, Eve did not draw this conclusion; instead, she ended her answer by saying that if either she or Adam ate or touched the tree's fruit, they would die. It is interesting to note that God had not previously prohibited Adam and Eve from "touching" the fruit. It seems, therefore, that Eve's response in fact reinforced God's prohibition: it would be dangerous even to approach the forbidden tree for fear of touching it, much less eating its fruit. Eve was quite literally circumscribing the forbidden tree, which stood in the middle of the garden.

This left the serpent little choice. If Eve took God's prohibition seriously, it would have not only to counter the threat God posed but also promise something more. This the serpent did, as I indicated earlier, by first dismissing God's threat and then promising the surpassing reward of divinity if she tasted the fruit.

Had the serpent only ridiculed God's threat, without extolling the alleged positive effects of eating the forbidden fruit, I assume that its challenge to God would have been less ominous. But perceiving that innocuous questions, or just dismissal of the threat, would probably not suffice to tempt Eve, the serpent felt compelled to make as airtight a case as possible.

The serpent indeed was persuasive, as the Bible reports. Eve not only was attracted to the fruit and ate it herself, but she also gave some to Adam, who ate it too. (In section 2.6 I shall analyze the game played between her and Adam over his eating of the fruit.)

To model the game played between Eve and the serpent, I assume that the serpent's best outcome (4) occurs when Eve eats the fruit without being tempted, because the serpent does nothing to defy God. (Although not a player in this game, God obviously is a determining force in the structuring of payoffs to the players.) The serpent's worst outcome (1), on the other hand, occurs when Eve resists

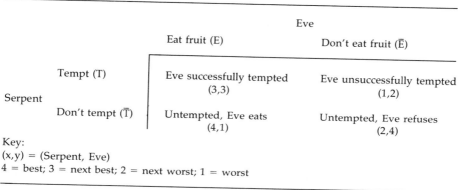

		Eve	
		Eat fruit (E)	Don't eat fruit (Ē)
Serpent	Tempt (T)	Eve successfully tempted (3,3)	Eve unsuccessfully tempted (1,2)
	Don't tempt (T̄)	Untempted, Eve eats (4,1)	Untempted, Eve refuses (2,4)

Key:
(x,y) = (Serpent, Eve)
4 = best; 3 = next best; 2 = next worst; 1 = worst

Figure 2.4 Outcome matrix for temptation game

its temptation, because the serpent's challenge to God's authority is unsuccessful. Between successfully tempting Eve—and defying God—and not even trying to entice a resolutely God-fearing Eve, I assume that the serpent would prefer the former outcome (3) to the latter (2). A confrontation with God, though serious, might be minimized, because God had not specifically forbidden the serpent to approach Eve. Moreover, the serpent, which had seen the naked Adam and Eve, may well have been overcome by a lust for Eve that overrode its apprehensions about challenging God's authority.[5]

Having justified the serpent's ranking of the outcomes in the matrix of figure 2.4, I shall now try to show that Eve's preferences for these outcomes were partially coincidental, partially conflictual.

Thus, unlike the previous game played between God, and Adam and Eve, over the imposition of constraints, the present game is not one of total conflict. I shall call games in which the preferences of the players are neither diametrically opposed nor fully coincidental *games of partial conflict.*

The outcome, I belive, that Eve and the serpent agreed on in the temptation game they played was the one next best for each: the successful enticement of Eve by the serpent [(3,3) in the outcome matrix of figure 2.4]. They were at cross-purposes, on the other hand, with respect to Eve's eating the fruit without being tempted: this would be the best outcome for the serpent (4), as I argued earlier, but the worst outcome (1) for Eve, for she would have defied God without good reason. Eve's next-worst outcome (2)

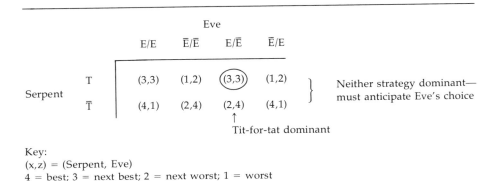

Figure 2.5 Payoff matrix for temptation game

would be to resist the temptation of the serpent, which presumably would have been extremely difficult for her. Eve's best outcome (4), I assume, would be not to face temptation in the first place, and then decide on her own to accede to God's request.

As the serpent had the first move, and only then did Eve respond, this game, like the previous one (and several others to follow) is properly modeled as a 2 × 4 game, with Eve having four strategies that depend on the serpent's prior choice of one or the other of its two strategies. The payoff matrix for this partial-conflict game is shown in figure 2.5 and reveals Eve to have a dominant strategy of tit-for-tat (E/Ē: eat if tempted, otherwise don't eat). If the serpent anticipated this strategy choice, then clearly it should tempt

Eve, for this strategy yields it a higher payoff (3) than not tempting Eve (2) in Eve's E/Ē column. Hence, the rational outcome of this game is the outcome that actually occurred, as in the constraint game. But it is an outcome whose consequences Eve immediately tried to downplay in God's eyes by making Adam an accessory to her sin.

2.6 Eve's Offer to Adam

The Bible is terse in its description of what followed after Eve ate the forbidden fruit:

She also gave some to her husband, and he ate. Then the eyes of both of them were opened and they perceived that they were naked; and they sewed together fig leaves and made themselves loin-cloths. (Gen. 3:6–7)

Previously, after Eve had been formed from one of Adam's ribs but before her temptation by the serpent, the Bible says:

The two of them were naked, the man and his wife, yet they felt no shame. (Gen. 2:25)

Evidently, if the eyes of Adam and Eve were opened upon eating the forbidden fruit—as the serpent had predicted they would be—their opening did not exactly make Adam and Eve divine. Instead, their nakedness became shameful as a consequence of their sin against God.

There follows a curious interplay among Adam, Eve, and God:

They [Adam and Eve] heard the sound of the LORD God moving about in the garden at the breezy time of day; and the man and his wife hid from the LORD God among the trees of the garden. The LORD God called out to the man and said to him, "Where are you?" He replied, "I heard the sound of You in the garden, and I was afraid because I was naked, so I hid." Then He asked, "Who told you that you were naked? Did you eat of the tree which I had forbidden you to eat?" The man said, "The woman You put at my side—she gave me of the tree, and I ate." And the LORD God said to the woman, "What is this you have done!" The woman replied, "The serpent duped me, and I ate." (Gen. 3:8–13)

God then condemns the serpent to crawl and eat dirt for the rest of its life, Eve to suffer pain in childbirth and to have her husband, whom she is attracted to, rule over her, and Adam to labor hard for his food and to return to the ground as dust.

The passage just quoted says several things:

1. By trying to hide from God, Adam and Eve clearly reveal their guilt.
2. If God could not find them in the garden, either He is not all-knowing or He is playing a game with Adam (man).
3. If God is playing a game, its purpose seems to be to elicit a confession from Adam, which He does.
4. Adam's confession, however, implicates Eve, who in turn implicates the serpent.

Doubtless, these sequential choices could be modeled as a formal game, but I think what is happening is reasonably clear without formalization. Adam and Eve, having sinned, make the ostensibly rational choice of trying to hide from God. To a certain extent they succeed, if God is truly confounded, but in the end, of course, the truth comes out. However, not willing to take all the blame, Adam acts rationally to share it with Eve, and Eve in turn is understandably willing to say she was duped by the serpent.

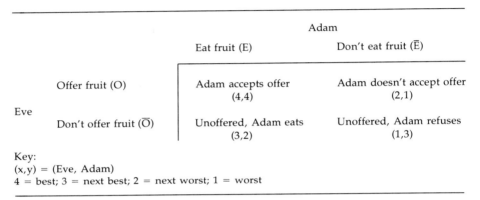

	Adam	
	Eat fruit (E)	Don't eat fruit (Ē)
Offer fruit (O)	Adam accepts offer (4,4)	Adam doesn't accept offer (2,1)
Eve Don't offer fruit (Ō)	Unoffered, Adam eats (3,2)	Unoffered, Adam refuses (1,3)

Key:
(x,y) = (Eve, Adam)
4 = best; 3 = next best; 2 = next worst; 1 = worst

Figure 2.6 Outcome matrix for sharing game

Spreading out the blame seems in retrospect a moderately successful strategy, because the lives of all the players are spared. Since God retreated from His earlier threat to kill all who ate the forbidden fruit, I conclude that Adam and Eve acted fairly intelligently. The serpent I am not so sure about; but given its preferences, I would submit that it acted rationally, too, though it is never heard from again. Judging from the serpent's previous behavior, though, I would guess that, like Adam and Eve, it would have temporized if it had had the opportunity.

Given the rather unfortunate turn of events precipitated by eating the forbidden fruit, the question I want to raise is why Adam accepted the fruit from Eve. Surely he could have anticipated that God would not be pleased if he defied His prohibition.

Moreover, Adam did not have to resist the temptation of a very cunning snake.

The explanation, I believe, lies in Adam's desire to remain unrestrained and his love for Eve. The first motive is evident from the constraint game. If this motive were also reinforced by love for Eve, then when Eve gave him the forbidden fruit, he could not easily refuse, despite the severity of the penalty for defiance that God had announced.

To make this argument more precise, consider Adam's ranking of the outcomes from best to worst as shown in the matrix of figure 2.6: he most wanted to remain unrestrained and please Eve by accepting her offer of the fruit once she had eaten it (4); if, however, she did not offer the fruit, he still valued his freedom (3); he would have been unhappy, though, if she did not offer fruit which he then ate (2); worst for him would be for her to have offered him fruit which he did not eat (1).

Eve, I assume, agreed with Adam about the top outcome (4)—for her to offer the fruit, and for him to eat it. Even if she did not offer it, however, she would have preferred (3) that he eat the fruit. If Adam had refused her offer, she would have been quite distressed (2), but worst (1) for Eve would be not even to try to offer fruit which Adam would subsequently refuse. In the latter case, Eve might forever blame herself for Adam's refusal to eat fruit which she never offered him.

Despite the apparent love of Adam and Eve for each other, their game is one of partial conflict. However, its proper representation as a 2 × 4 game, in which Eve has the first move, shows Adam to have a dominant strategy of tit-for-tat (E/$\overline{\text{E}}$): eat the fruit if Eve offers it, otherwise don't eat it (see figure 2.7). Given this strategy choice by Adam, Eve's best choice is to offer the fruit (O), which yields both players their best outcome.

Although these are the choices Adam and Eve actually made, it may seem strange to consider the resulting outcome their "best." Nevertheless, I would contend that not only were their choices rational, but it is fair to call Adam's acceptance of Eve's offer of the fruit "best," given their strong will to be unrestrained and their presumed love for each other.

This view is supported by the fact that if Eve had (irrationally) chosen not to offer the fruit ($\overline{\text{O}}$), Adam's subsequent best response would have been either $\overline{\text{E}}$/$\overline{\text{E}}$ or E/$\overline{\text{E}}$, as seen from the payoff matrix of figure 2.7. In either case, it would have been rational for Adam not to eat the fruit, resulting in his next-best outcome (3) and Eve's worst (1).

Given their desire for independence and love for each other, however, would it really have been better for Eve not to offer the fruit, and Adam to let Eve face the consequences of her sin alone? I think not: knowing Adam's preferences, it was clearly rational for Eve to offer the fruit, and then for Adam to accept it.

But for argument's sake, assume that Eve, having succumbed to the wiles of the serpent, most wanted Adam *not* to follow her bad example. Her love for Adam, and her wish not to drag him into sin, moved her to desire most the outcome in which she did not offer the fruit and he did not accept it. This assumption about Eve's most-preferred outcome changes (1,3) into (4,3) in the outcome and payoff matrices of figures 2.6 and 2.7.

If Adam's preference ordering remains unchanged, then he still has a dominant strategy of tit-for-tat.

		Adam			
		E/E	Ē/Ē	E/Ē	Ē/E
Eve	O	(4,4)	(2,1)	((4,4))	(2,1)
	Ō	(3,2)	(1,3)	(1,3)	(3,2)

} Neither strategy dominant—
must anticipate Adam's choice

↑
Tit-for-tat dominant

Key:
(x,y) = (Eve, Adam)
4 = best; 3 = next best; 2 = next worst; 1 = worst
Circled outcome rational

Figure 2.7 Payoff matrix for sharing game

Now, however, Eve, anticipating Adam's dominant strategy choice, would choose not to offer the fruit, whatever her lower-ranking preferences were. Adam would not eat the fruit, and the resulting (4,3) outcome would be best for Eve, next best for Adam.

The problem with this new game is that the rational outcome it predicts is not the outcome that occurred in the Bible. I conclude, therefore, that if the players were rational and had complete information about each other's preferences, Eve did not believe in self-denial to save Adam. Instead, her love took the more selfish form of wanting to share the fruit with Adam, and so she offered it to him. (Adam's preferences were also selfish in rendering his strategy of tit-for-tat dominant.) If Eve knew at the point of offering that she had been duped by the serpent and had sinned—which is not entirely clear—her love for Adam did not extend to trying to protect him.

Most probable, perhaps, is that Eve did not fully understand the consequences of her action at that point and simply wanted to please Adam. Given she knew his preferences, this suggests an unselfish Eve. Adam, under this interpretation, wanted to show his gratitude by accepting the fruit. Whether selfish or selfless, Adam and Eve's act was in palpable defiance of God's edict.

2.7 The Punishment of Adam and Eve

I described in section 2.6 the punishment God inflicted on the serpent for tempting Eve and defying

His authority, and on Adam and Eve for ignoring His threat by eating from the tree of knowledge of good and bad. After announcing His punishment, God made clear why the knowledge so gained from eating the fruit of this tree posed a problem:

Now that man has become like one of us, knowing good and bad, what if he should stretch out his hand and take also from the tree of life and eat, and live forever! (Gen. 3:22)

In other words, man, having become divine in his ability to distinguish good from bad, as the serpent had predicted would happen, could perhaps threaten God's authority if he also gained immortality from eating from the tree of life. Consequently, God chose His only viable alternative:

So the LORD God banished him [man] from the garden of Eden, to till the soil from which he was taken. He drove the man out, and stationed east of the garden of Eden the cherubim and the fiery ever-turning sword, to guard the way to the tree of life. (Gen. 3:23–24)

Thereby the hierarchy with God on top was established, which presumably was His best outcome under the circumstances.

I say "under the circumstances" because if Adam and Eve had not eaten from the tree of knowledge of good and bad, God presumably would not have felt the need to banish them from the garden of Eden.[6] Banishment became God's rational choice only after Adam and Eve came to know good and bad. If they had not acquired this knowledge by eating the forbidden fruit, then the fruit of the tree of life would not have rendered them a threat: immortality alone—without knowledge of good and bad—would be an uninformed and, presumably, impotent presence. It was, apparently, the combination of immortality and knowledge that God considered intolerable, so he took the appropriate measure to arrest the immortality of an already knowledgeable Adam and Eve and thereby ensure His own unique and privileged position.[7]

This calculation is quite straightforward and therefore does not, in my opinion, require any more formal elaboration. What seems more problematic is why God did not carry out the punishment for eating the forbidden fruit—death—with which He had previously threatened Adam and Eve.

The explanation, I believe, lies in the fact that Adam, after a brief attempt at evasion, admitted his guilt. Moreover, as I indicated in section 2.6, both he and Eve pleaded extenuating circumstances, which seem to have been accepted, for the Bible does not report the serpent as entering a counterplea in its defense.

More formally, Adam and Eve may be viewed initially as choosing between obeying or disobeying God. (See game tree in figure 2.8.) After they disobeyed God and ate the forbidden fruit, God interrogated Adam, who could either deny his guilt or admit it; in the latter case, I assume, Adam would try to present good reasons for his defiance of God. Face to face with a death penalty, a bald admission of guilt would not be a strategy choice Adam would seriously entertain.

God, it seems, after Adam had made a choice, could choose from among three responses: kill Adam and Eve, as promised; punish but not kill them; or ignore their disobedience. In figure 2.8, I assume the latter course of action would result in God's worst outcome (1); it would be humiliating for God to ignore Adam and Eve's defiance of His threat and henceforth be considered weak. In ascending order of preference, I assume God would next most prefer a denial of guilt that He recognized as mendacious and for which He would presumably kill Adam and Eve (2); then an admission of guilt for which He also would kill them, despite Eve's apparent deception by the serpent (3); then to punish them, short of death, for their disobedience (4);

and, finally, to have them obey Him by not eating the forbidden fruit in the first place (5).

Adam and Eve's preferences, I assume, ascend from being killed for their disobedience after admitting their guilt (1); unsuccessfully denying their guilt, with death presumably as a consequence of their mendacity (2); obeying God (3); being punished but not killed for disobedience after admitting their guilt (4); and not being punished for disobedience (5). Most controversial, probably, is my ranking obedience only in the middle ("Adam and Eve faithful, God pleased"), below punishment for disobedience ("Adam and Eve honest, God evenhanded"). This I do because I believe that Eve, after hearing the persuasive arguments of the serpent, and Adam, after being offered the fruit by the woman he presumably loved, did not feel seriously threatened in eating the fruit of the tree of knowledge of good and bad. In their perception at the time of choice, disobedience of God, despite its risks, seemed less fearsome when considered in light of the ultimate reward of becoming godlike together.

God, one must remember, had not previously threatened anybody—and therefore had not been unsuccessfully challenged. Since the credibility of His word had not been established, as it was to be

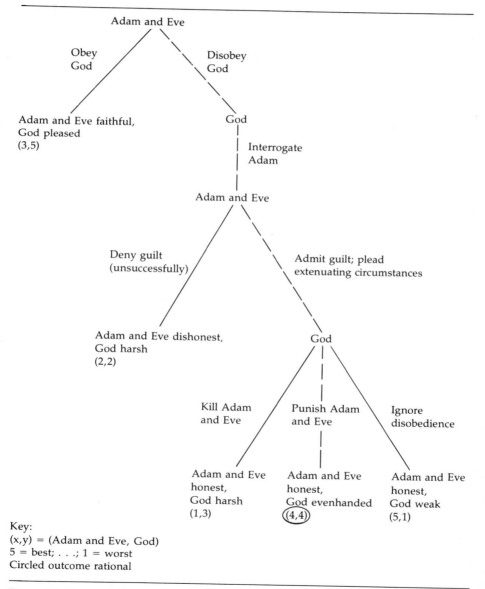

Key:
(x,y) = (Adam and Eve, God)
5 = best; . . .; 1 = worst
Circled outcome rational

Figure 2.8 Game tree for punishment game

later, Adam and Eve were perhaps justified in not taking His threat completely at face value. Besides, to become divine by eating the forbidden fruit, as the serpent promised, was no mean thing.

I could write down the matrix form of the game tree of figure 2.8 in a manner similar to that in which the game tree of figure 2.2 was translated into the payoff matrix of figure 2.3 in the constraint game. However, as both players have more strategies to juggle than they do in this and previous games, the matrix form becomes somewhat complex and cumbersome. Besides, choices that rational players would make can be read off directly from the game tree, so it is unnecessary to work from the matrix form to determine the rational outcome. (There are, nonetheless, advantages to using the matrix form that I will discuss in section 3.2.)

The determination of rational choices from the game tree is based on a backward reasoning process. One asks first what the last-moving player (God) would choose if play got to his choice point (or *move*) at the bottom of the tree. Since God's best choice *at this point* is to punish Adam and Eve (4), I assume He would choose this strategy if play got to this move. Therefore, I distinguish it with a dashed rather than a solid line.

Adam and Eve's prior choice is

between denying or admitting their guilt. If they admit their guilt, they know that God as a rational player would subsequently choose His punishment option associated with (4,4)—for reasons given in the previous paragraph—so this is the payoff they can reasonably associate with admitting their guilt. Between (2,2) and (4,4), Adam and Eve would prefer (4,4).

Working backward again, I have indicated with a vertical line God's interrogation of Adam. Since I assume this move by God not to involve any choice among possible alternatives, the next-prior choice a player has to make is that by Adam and Eve between obeying or disobeying God. Once again I associate the "rational" payoff (4,4) with their option (disobedience) that will eventually result in this payoff. Since Adam and Eve prefer it to (3,5) associated with obeying God, I assume disobedience is their rational choice.

Looking ahead now from their first move, and anticipating the future moves of all players (including themselves), Adam and Eve can conclude that their choice of disobedience will eventually lead to the circled outcome (4,4) at the bottom of the tree, given the rationality of all players at each move. Thus, the rational outcome of the game is found by assuming rational choices of each player at future choice points, mentally substituting the payoffs [only (4,4) in this game] associated with these choices for the branches at a prior move, and carrying this process backward to the first move of the game.

By this reasoning, the choices of disobedience by Adam and Eve, and punishment of them by God, are rational. Adam and Eve must anticipate the future choice of punishment short of death to justify their not obeying God, so they do not have a dominant, or unconditionally best, strategy.

Since God has no real strategy choice to make until the last move of the game, He has the easier task of maximizing only with respect to His three options at this point, which I call "harsh," "even-handed," and "weak" in figure 2.8. Effectively I assume that killing Adam and Eve, and thereby nullifying His grand design at the creation, is for God inferior to more lenient punishment of Adam and Eve that preserves His design. Some punishment is definitely called for, however, to avoid being considered "weak" and losing credibility in future games.

Thus, God's choice in the punishment game is partially dependent upon the choices He made at the creation. In addition, it seems plausible to assume that God knows that His choice will also set a precedent for His behavior in future

games. While there are other time-related interdependencies among the games I have analyzed so far, there is also sufficient independence among them, I believe, to make the individual games reasonable models of the choice situations they are meant to portray.

The major problem with this kind of analysis, perhaps, is knowing what game is being played: Who are its players? What are their sequential strategy choices? What are the possible outcomes of the game? How do the players evaluate these outcomes? Could, for example, Adam and Eve really anticipate punishment short of death in the punishment game, or that their sin would even be discovered by God? Should the serpent be included as a player in this game? I turn to these and related questions in a final consideration of games played at the beginning.

2.8 Conclusions

I have analyzed five games in this chapter:

1. The creation "game" (player: God).

2. The constraint game (players: God vs. Adam and Eve).

3. The temptation game (players: serpent vs. Eve).

4. The sharing game (players: Eve vs. Adam).

5. The punishment game (players: Adam and Eve vs. God).

I have put "game" in quotation marks in the case of the creation because it is a degenerate kind of game—a one-person *game against nature* in which God is the sole player. Such a game involves a player's choosing the best from a set of alternatives that "nature" provides. In the creation game, it will be recalled, God is not only a player but also the Supreme Being who incrementally builds up a world that becomes nature, with man as its centerpiece.

In this game, I suggested that God's introduction of man with free will into the world better satisfied His craving for respect and praise— genuinely motivated—than other alternatives. But it was risky: man, given his freedom, may not resist worldly temptations and act right-eously—that is, as God desires— particularly under trying circumstances. Nonetheless, if God also desired to relieve His boredom by making the world less predictable and therefore more exciting and challenging, as Kolakowski argued, then this risk of cutting man's puppet strings was probably worth taking.

Once past the creation, the risks of freewheeling human biblical characters are quickly driven home to God. Constraints on their free-dom that are rational for God to set up are immediately violated by Adam and Eve. The temptation game played between the serpent and Eve establishes the rationality of Adam's later capitulation. Fi-nally, the punishment game dem-onstrates that Adam and Eve should admit their guilt—pleading extenuating circumstances—and God should punish but not kill them.

In my opinion, the games I have analyzed in this chapter capture the essential elements of the various conflicts at the beginning and "feed into" each other in a logical way. Yet not only do their players over-lap, but the games also overlap in time; one does not necessarily end before another begins. For example, it is not unreasonable to suppose that when Eve plays the game with the serpent, she is also thinking about future possibilities of sharing the fruit with her husband and the possible punishment she might in-cur. Nonetheless, I have modeled these considerations in different discrete games.

This partitioning of games is ar-bitrary, as is any theoretical simpli-fication of a complex social situation in which not all the paremeters are well specified or known. If nothing else, the analysis demonstrates that the strategic situation is indeed complex—certainly more compli-cated than most traditional treatments of the Adam and Eve story suggest—which I believe* establishes the need for a framework within which biblical analysis can be carried out systematically.

In this story, as in those that follow, I do not pretend to offer the final word on how and why the players acted as they did. Unquestionably, there are other plausible game-theoretic treatments of this subject matter, including not just different preference assumptions but also different assumptions about the games played and their sequencing. It is hard to make a case for uniqueness in any post hoc organization of social reality.

A possible response to this problem of nonuniqueness is to try to construct one grand kind of game that encompasses all conceivable player choices at different points in time. The problem with such a construction is not only that the game would become hopelessly complex and therefore very difficult to analyze. A more serious problem is that it is highly unlikely that real human players, and perhaps even God, peer very far into the future and mentally juggle complex scenarios.[8] Even in the relatively simple punishment game, for example, it is not evident that Adam and Eve foresaw that God might soften His punishment if they explained to Him the problems they faced, and that they made this prevision the basis for admitting their guilt. It is a reasonable supposition, but by no means incontrovertible.

Be that as it may, I would submit that game theory provides an appropriate framework within which the present strategic analysis, if found wanting, can be modified or refined. One modification of preferences was suggested and rejected in the punishment game. In chapter 3 I shall show how several alternative interpretations of the preferences of the characters, when there is ambiguity, can be systematically investigated and assessed.

3

The Meaning of Faith

3.1 Introduction

In this chapter I shall show that Abraham's attempted sacrifice of his son, Isaac (as given in Genesis), and Jephthah's actual sacrifice of his daughter (as given in Judges), can be viewed as two-person games played by the fathers with God. Different interpretations of these games suggest that there is a trade-off between "faith" and "rationality": the more sophisticated the rationality calculations biblical characters make, the less need for them to have blind faith in God to achieve their goals. Thus, as the faith of a character wavers, his rationality may sustain him—but not necessarily if he deviates seriously and God is unsympathetic.

One conclusion I draw from these stories is that "rational" interpretations of biblical actions are no more farfetched than "faith" interpretations. In fact, I would argue that a more mundane, rational explanation, precisely because it does not

This chapter is based largely on Steven J. Brams, "Faith Versus Rationality in the Bible: Game-Theoretic Interpretations of Sacrifice in the Old Testament," paper delivered at the International Conference on Applied Game Theory, Vienna, June 13–16, 1978. The proceedings of this conference have been published as *Applied Game Theory: Proceedings of a Conference, Vienna 1978*, ed. St. J. Brams, A. Schotter, and G. Schwödiauer (Würzburg, West Germany: Physica-Verlag, 1980). I am grateful to Physica-Verlag for permission to use material from this paper.

assume of biblical characters super-human righteousness in the face of adversity, is more credible. This is not to say, however, that faith is irrational. On the contrary, being faithful means having preferences such that one's rational strategy is independent of the strategy of other players—that is, one's own values completely determine how one acts.

A second conclusion I draw from this analysis is that God can brook some deviance but not complete rejection. Knowing the failings of His subjects, He is capable of—but not always willing to demonstrate—mercy. This attitude of reasonable toleration, in my opinion, is consistent with conceptualizing God as a game player, omnipresent but not omnipotent, rational but not emotionless. With vastly scaled-down presence and power, He is thus not unlike most of us.

In the two stories of human sacrifice from the Old Testament that I shall analyze, God's motivations seem quite plain. Nevertheless, I shall consider alternative interpretations of His preferences, as well as alternative interpretations of the preference of His antagonists, in trying to model their behavior as that of players in a game. As the two stories have different outcomes, they show up nicely the dependence of game outcomes on player preferences. I shall conclude by comparing the game-theoretic explanations of player choices in these games with nonrational interpretations of these stories.

3.2 Abraham's Sacrifice

With characteristic economy of language, chapter 22 of Genesis begins, "Some time afterward, God put Abraham to the test." Then, in just eighteen verses, one of the greatest and most poignant stories from the Bible is told. The significance of this story, and its interlocking themes of faithfulness, sacrifice, and murder, have been subjected to prodigious analysis and interpretation, some of which I shall briefly discuss in section 3.4.

In the story, God commands Abraham:

Take your son, your favored one, Isaac, whom you love, and go to the land Moriah, and offer him there as a burnt offering on one of the heights which I will point out to you. (Gen. 22:2)

Faithful servant of God that he is, Abraham sets out on his ass with Isaac, accompanied by two of his men with firewood for the sacrifice.

On the third day of the journey, Abraham sees the place for the sacrifice and leaves his ass and two men behind. He gives Isaac the firewood to carry, and he himself carries the firestone and the knife.

When Isaac asks, "Here are the fire-stone and the wood; but where is the sheep for the burnt offering?" (Gen. 22:7), Abraham answers, "God will see to the sheep for His burnt offering, my son" (Gen. 22:8).

Abraham builds an altar and lays out the wood, after which he binds Isaac and lays him on the altar on top of the wood. As he picks up his knife to kill his son,

an angel of the LORD called to him from heaven: "Abraham! Abraham!" And he answered, "Here I am." And he said, "Do not raise your hand against the boy, or do anything to him. For now I know that you fear God, since you have not withheld your son, your favored one, from Me." When Abraham looked up, his eye fell upon a ram, caught in the thicket by its horns. So Abraham went and took the ram and offered it up as a burnt offering in place of his son. (Gen. 22:11–13)

Abraham is then rewarded for his faithfulness when the angel calls from heaven a second time:

By Myself I swear, the LORD declares: because you have done this and have not withheld your son, your favored one, I will bestow My blessing upon you and make your descendants as numerous as the stars of heaven and the sands on the sea-shore; and your descendants shall seize the gates of their foes. All the nations on earth shall bless themselves by your descendants, because you have obeyed My command. (Gen. 22:16–18)

If this game is viewed as played between Abraham and God, Abraham has two strategy choices:

1. Offer Isaac: O.
2. Don't offer Isaac: $\overline{O}$.

God, in turn, has two strategy choices:

1. Renege (if Isaac offered)/relent (if not): R.
2. Don't renege/relent: $\overline{R}$.

God's first choice is a cooperative response, implying—whatever Abraham does—that He intended just to test him. On the other hand, God's second choice would indicate that He was deadly serious about His command to sacrifice Isaac. The consequences of these strategy choices for both players are summarized verbally in the outcome matrix shown in figure 3.1. For example, if Abraham does not attempt to sacrifice Isaac, and God is unmerciful, Isaac's fate (as well as Abraham's) is uncertain (see figure 3.1).

Since God's moves occurred after Abraham's, in full knowledge of Abraham's strategy choice (O or $\overline{O}$), the proper representation of this

		God			
		Renege (if Isaac offered)/ relent (if not): R		Don't renege/relent: $\overline{\text{R}}$	
Abraham	Offer Isaac: O	Abraham faithful, God merciful, Isaac saved	a. (4,4) b. (4,4) c. (4,4)	Abraham faithful, God adamant, Isaac sacrificed	a. (3,3) b. (2,3) c. (1,3)
	Don't offer Isaac: $\overline{\text{O}}$	Abraham resistant, God merciful, Isaac saved	a. (2,1) b. (3,1) c. (3,1)	Abraham resistant, God adamant, Isaac's fate uncertain	a. (1,2) b. (1,2) c. (2,2)

Key:

(x,y) = (Abraham, God)

4 = best; 3 = next best; 2 = next worst; 1 = worst

a. *Abraham faithful regardless*: prefers "offer" over "don't offer"

b. *Abraham wavers somewhat*: prefers God "renege/relent" over "don't renege/relent"

c. *Abraham wavers seriously*: Isaac's life paramount—same as (b) above except if God adamant, would prefer "don't offer"

Figure 3.1 Outcome matrix for Abraham's sacrifice

game in matrix form is as a 2 × 4 game (Abraham has two strategies, God has four), which I shall analyze shortly. For the purpose of evaluating the four possible outcomes that can occur, however, the 2 × 2 form will be used.

As in chapter 2, I shall attempt in my evaluation to rank, but not attach numerical values to, the outcomes for each player from best to worst, with "4" being best and "1" worst. I assume God prefers that Abraham show his faith by offering Isaac, so OR and O$\overline{\text{R}}$ in the first row of the outcome matrix of figure 3.1 are His two most-preferred outcomes. Given Abraham chooses O,

I assume that God would prefer to put Abraham to the test (R)—as the Bible says He intends—and not allow Isaac actually to be sacrificed ($\overline{\text{R}}$), so for God OR = 4 and O$\overline{\text{R}}$ = 3. If Abraham should not offer Isaac ($\overline{\text{O}}$), however, I assume that God would prefer not to relent, so $\overline{\text{O}}$$\overline{\text{R}}$ = 2 and $\overline{\text{O}}$R = 1. Given these assumptions, I now want to show what consequences they have for the rational play of the game when Abraham's faith wavers.

In the key to figure 3.1, and in figure 3.2, I have briefly characterized three different assumptions about Abraham's preference rankings. Also in figure 3.2, I have given

a. *Abraham faithful regardless*: whatever God chooses subsequently—renege/relent (R) or not (R̄)—Abraham prefers to offer (O).

		God		God			
		R	R̄	R/R	R̄/R̄	R/R̄	R̄/R
Abraham	O	(4,4)	(3,3)	(4,4)	(3,3)	(4,4)ⓞ	(3,3)	←- Offer dominant
	Ō	(2,1)	(1,2)	(2,1)	(1,2)	(1̄,2)	(2,1)

Tit-for-tat dominant

b. *Abraham wavers somewhat*: whatever Abraham chooses—offer (O) or don't offer (Ō)—he prefers God subsequently renege/relent (R).

		God		God			
		R	R̄	R/R	R̄/R̄	R/R̄	R̄/R
Abraham	O	(4,4)	(2,3)	(4,4)	(2,3)	(4,4)ⓞ	(2,3)
	Ō	(3,1)	(1,2)	(3,1)	(1,2)	(1̄,2)	(3,1)

Neither strategy dominant— must anticipate God's choice

Tit-for-tat dominant

c. *Abraham wavers seriously*: same as (b) above, except given God is adamant (R̄), Abraham prefers not to offer (Ō).

		God		God			
		R	R̄	R/R	R̄/R̄	R/R̄	R̄/R
Abraham	O	(4,4)	(1,3)	(4,4)	(1,3)	(4,4)ⓞ	(1,3)
	Ō	(3,1)	(2,2)	(3,1)	(2,2)	(2̄,2)	(3,1)

Neither strategy dominant— must anticipate God's choice

Tit-for-tat dominant

Key:
(x,y) = (Abraham, God)
4 = best; 3 = next best; 2 = next worst; 1 = worst
Circled outcome rational

Figure 3.2 Payoff matrices for Abraham's sacrifice

the proper 2 × 4 normal-form representation of the game. It reflects the fact that since Abraham has the first move, he can choose either to offer or not offer Isaac. God, on the other hand, whose moves occur only after Abraham has made a choice, has four possible strategy choices, depending on what Abraham chooses:

1. R/R *Be merciful regardless:* Renege if Isaac offered, relent if not.

2. $\overline{R}/\overline{R}$ *Be adamant regardless:* Don't renege if Isaac offered, don't relent if not.

3. R/$\overline{R}$ *Tit-for-tat:* Renege if Isaac offered, don't relent if not.

4. $\overline{R}$/R *Tat-for-tit:* Don't renege if Isaac offered, relent if not.

Like the game tree for the constraint game given in figure 2.8, game trees could be constructed for the different assumptions about Abraham's preferences. Using the "backward rationality" argument applied to the more complex punishment game tree of figure 2.8, rational outcomes could then be determined for each preference assumption, instead of looking for dominant strategies in the 2 × 4 payoff matrices in figure 3.2.

However, I prefer to analyze the payoff matrices for two reasons: (1) they are not complex; and (2) they reveal immediately whether one player has a dominant strategy or both do, and thus whether contingent strategic calculations must be made by a player in the game. In the game tree, one cannot discern this possible dependence without first doing the backward rationality calculations; hence, interdependent calculations are more easily highlighted by the matrix form. On the other hand, when there are more than two players, or two strategy choices at a move, the payoff matrix quickly becomes cumbersome and the game-tree analysis is easier. Thus, I shall move back and forth between matrix analysis and tree analysis of games, depending on their complexity.

What meaning can be attached to the three different preference assumptions for Abraham? As I indicate in figure 3.2, it seems reasonable to assume that Abraham may (a) be faithful regardless, (b) waver somewhat, or (c) waver seriously. Operationally, these assumptions have the following interpretations:

a. Whatever God chooses subsequently, Abraham prefers to offer Isaac (O). Of course, Abraham would prefer that God renege on His demand that Isaac be sacrificed (R), so OR = 4 and O$\overline{R}$ = 3, which makes God and Abraham's first two preferences identical. If Abraham does not offer Isaac ($\overline{O}$), he would prefer to do so when God relents (R) and Isaac is thereby saved, so $\overline{O}R = 2$ and $\overline{O}\,\overline{R} = 1$ for Abraham.

b. Whatever Abraham chooses, he prefers that God subsequently renege/relent (R). Since Abraham would prefer to show his faith by offering Isaac (O), $OR = 4$ and $\overline{O}R = 3$. If God is adamant ($\overline{R}$), however, Abraham would prefer to offer Isaac (O) as a show of his faith, so $O\overline{R} = 2$ and $\overline{O}\,\overline{R} = 1$.

c. Same as (b) above, except now, given God is adamant ($\overline{R}$), Abraham would prefer not to offer Isaac ($\overline{O}$)—perhaps hoping that this will save his son's life, even if he himself is punished—so $\overline{O}\,\overline{R} = 2$ and $O\overline{R} = 1$. This assumption says, in effect, that Isaac's life is paramount—Abraham's worst outcome occurs when Isaac is offered and God does not arrest his sacrifice.

What are the game-theoretic implications of these different preference assumptions I have posited for Abraham? Notice, first, that in the case of all three 2 × 4 payoff matrices in figure 3.2, God's tit-for-tat strategy is dominant, or unconditionally best. Only under assumption (a), however, does Abraham also have a dominant strategy: to offer Isaac. The intersection of Abraham's dominant strategy (O) and God's dominant strategy ($R/\overline{R}$) yields the best outcome [(4,4)] for both players. Of course, this was

the outcome that was actually chosen in the game.

The best outcome for both players under assumptions (b) and (c) are also (4,4), but a wavering Abraham in these cases no longer has a straightforward choice. Rather, since he does not have a dominant strategy under assumptions (b) and (c), Abraham must anticipate the strategy God will choose in order to determine his own best choice.

What strategy, then, will God as a rational player choose? Since God's tit-for-tat strategy of $R/\overline{R}$ remains dominant under assumptions (b) and (c), I assume He will choose it. Anticipating God's choice of tit-for-tat, Abraham in both cases would obtain a higher payoff (4) by choosing O rather than $\overline{O}$, which would yield him payoffs of 1 and 2, respectively, under assumptions (b) and (c).

If rational, then, Abraham will presumably choose O. The choice of O by Abraham, and $R/\overline{R}$ by God, once again results in both players' obtaining their best outcome of (4,4); now, however, the process by which it is arrived at is different. Specifically, a wavering Abraham under preference assumptions (b) and (c) must first anticipate God's rational (dominant) strategy choice before he can decide what is best for himself. Under assumption (a), by contrast, Abraham has no need to make such a calculation since he himself has a dominant strategy—a best choice not conditional on what God might subsequently choose—and hence can act rationally without knowing anything about God's preferences and the choices they might entail.

The conclusion I draw from this analysis of Abraham's sacrifice is that faith in God may ease the often difficult choices biblical characters face. Faith, at least in Abraham's case, meant that he did not have to consider God's possible reactions to his own best course of action, which was to obey God.

To obey God blindly is, in fact, to act *as if* one has a dominant strategy—an unconditionally best choice—that requires no detailed preference information about the other player, much less an anticipation of what strategy he might choose. On the other hand, when a character's faith in God is not blind, he needs to make more sophisticated calculations to ascertain how to act rationally. Although his strategy choice may be the same in either case, the logical process needed to arrive at it in the second case will be more demanding in terms of both the preference information required and the sophistication needed to process this information.

To argue that Abraham indeed acted rationally, it is important to ascertain that he knew, or had some inkling of, God's preferences in the three games I have postulated he might have played. To be sure, in the case of preference assumption (a) for Abraham, it does not matter whether Abraham knows God's preferences, for he has a dominant strategy that is by definition rational whatever strategy God subsequently chooses. But it does matter that Abraham know God's preferences in the case of assumptions (b) and (c) to play rationally the games that these assumptions define. Actually, however, for a somewhat or seriously wavering Abraham, it is sufficient that he believe God's attitude to be either forgiving regardless (R/R) or tit-for-tat (R/$\overline{R}$), for both these attitudes imply Abraham should offer Isaac (O).

In my opinion, there is good reason for Abraham to harbor such beliefs. On several previous occasions, God had been magnanimous with Abraham, telling him, among other things,

I will make of you a great nation;
And I will bless you;
I will make your name great;
And you shall be a blessing. (Gen. 12:2)

I will make your offspring as the dust of the earth, so that if one can count the dust of the earth, then your offspring too can be counted. (Gen. 13:16)

"Look toward heaven and count the stars, if you are able to count them." And He added: "So shall your offspring be." (Gen. 15:5)

I make you the father of a multitude of nations. I will make you exceedingly fertile, and make nations of you; and kings shall come forth from you. I will maintain My covenant between Me and you, and your offspring to come, as an everlasting covenant throughout the ages, to be God to you and to your offspring to come. (Gen. 17:5-7)

Speaking of Abraham's wife, Sarai (later Sarah), who had been barren for many years, God said to Abraham:

I will bless her; indeed, I will give you a son by her. I will bless her so that she shall give rise to nations; rulers of peoples shall issue from her. (Gen. 17:16)

The son, of course, was Isaac, whom Sarah bore at the age of ninety (Abraham was then one hundred). God further said:

I will maintain My covenant with him as an everlasting covenant for his offspring to come. (Gen. 17:19)

Given all these assurances, is it conceivable that Abraham could have believed that God meant him to sacrifice Isaac, the progenitor-to-be of multitudinous offspring?

My answer is that it is conceivable, given the steadfastly righteous—and perhaps gullible—man that Abraham was. But it is also conceivable that Abraham suspected that he was only being tested and made the calculation that, in that event, it was rational for him to offer Isaac.

That Abraham was not above this kind of thinking is illustrated by a story in his earlier life in which he passed off Sarah as his sister. Because of Sarah's great beauty, Abraham feared that if it were known that he was her husband, he would be killed by the Egyptians so that Pharaoh could take Sarah as his wife.[1] In fact, Pharaoh did take Sarah as his wife under this misrepresentation, but when the truth came out after misfortunes to Pharaoh, he angrily ordered the dissembling couple out of Egypt.

I offer this background information to make the point that while it is hard to say exactly what game Abraham was playing, it is certainly not impossible to imagine that Abraham knew something about God's preferences and hence was aware that he was indeed a player in a game. The three games I have posited all offer, in my view, plausible game-theoretic explanations for Abraham's sacrificial offering of Isaac to God. One is based on the blind faith of an unswerving Abraham; the other two, on the more sophisticated calculations of a concerned father. Since all games dictate the same rational choice for Abraham (O), they do not really test the "blindness" of Abraham's faith.

Thus, although God's harrowing test of Abraham succeeds in establishing that Abraham will obey His command—however ghastly—Abraham may well have done so for reasons other than faith. Hence, God's test does not assuredly dispel doubts about Abraham's faith, given Abraham knows God's preferences and is rational. I shall next show that in another sacrificial game with a different outcome, faith *is* distinguishable from a more sophisticated game-theoretic rationality for one wavering assumption but not the other.

3.3 Jephthah's Sacrifice

As told in chapter 11 of Judges, Jephthah, an able warrior and the son of a prostitute, was driven from his home in Gilead by the legitimate sons of his father. In the country of Tob where he settled, "men of low character gathered about Jephthah and went out raiding with him" (Judg. 11:3). The elders of Gilead, however, faced by an Ammonite attack, recalled him and sought his aid, which he consented to give on condition they appoint him commander of Gilead after his victory.

The elders agreed, and Jephthah then tried to negotiate with the Ammonites, but the negotiations got nowhere. Forced into battle, Jephthah made the following vow to the LORD:

If you deliver the Ammonites into my hands, then whatever comes out of the door of my house to meet me on my safe return from the Ammonites shall be the LORD's and shall be offered by me as a burnt offering. (Judg. 11:30–31)

Having made this fateful vow, Jephthah routed the Ammonites, who then submitted to the Israelites. Upon returning to his home, Jephthah, to his utter dismay, was greeted by his daughter and only child "with timbrel and dance" (Judg. 11:34)! His heart broken, Jephthah rent his clothes and told his daughter, "I have uttered a vow to the LORD and I cannot retract" (Judg. 11:35).

Resigned to her fate, Jephthah's daughter dolefully asked that her sacrifice be postponed for two months so that, with her companions, she could "lament upon the hills and there bewail my maidenhood" (Judg. 11:37). Jephthah granted her this wish, but at the end of this period he grimly fulfilled his vow. The Bible reports that it henceforth became a custom in Israel for maidens to commemorate this tragic event by chanting dirges for the daughter of Jephthah during an annual four-day mourning period.

In Jephthah's case, God clearly was not in a mood for testing but instead played for keeps. But what does this say about His preferences, and how does this translate into choices He and Jephthah made in the game they played?

I would suggest that there are at least two interpretations that can be made of God's preferences in this game. One I call *show-of-faith*; the other, *vindictive*. In the case of Abraham's sacrifice, it will be recalled, God preferred that Abraham show his faith by offering to sacrifice Isaac, but given that he did, God preferred to renege on His demand. Now, in the show-of-faith interpretation, I assume that God prefers that Jephthah offer his daughter and thereby fulfill his vow; but, given that Jephthah offers his daughter, I assume that God prefers to allow the sacrifice to be consummated (see figure 3.3). Note that the only difference between these games and those shown in figure 3.2 is that "4" and "3" for God are interchanged in the first rows of the payoff matrices.

Why this change in God's mood? Since Abraham's time, the Israelites had caused God much grief, both before and after the conquest of Canaan (discussed in chapters 5 and 7); consequently, God was not inclined to be sympathetic with people like Jephthah who were too quick to make solemn vows. Whether Jephthah could anticipate this problem or only remembered the test of Abraham is hard to say. (Since it is believed that Jephthah's story was written before Abraham's, however, it is questionable whether precedents are even meaningful here.) In any event, to carry out the subsequent analysis, I shall assume that Jephthah anticipated that God might be less than sympathetic with his situation, for I have already analyzed in the Abraham story the consequences that flow from a more benign view of God's intent.

I assume three different preference orderings for Jephthah that duplicate those of Abraham given earlier: (a) faithful regardless; (b) wavers somewhat; and (c) wavers seriously. These different interpretations of Jephthah's preferences are shown in figure 3.3 for the show-of-faith interpretation of God's preferences described previously.

Under the three different interpretations of Jephthah's preferences, God has a dominant strategy of don't renege/relent regardless. Observe that by making the out-

a. *Jephthah faithful regardless*: whatever God chooses subsequently—renege/relent (R) or not (R̄)—Jephthah prefers to offer (O).

		God		God			
		R	R̄	R/R	R̄/R̄	R/R̄	R̄/R
Jephthah	O	(4,3)	(3,4)	(4,3)	ⓐ(3,4)	(4,3)	(3,4)	← Offer dominant
	Ō	(2,1)	(1,2)	(2,1)	(1̄,2)	(1,2)	(2,1)

↑
Don't renege/relent regardless dominant

b. *Jephthah wavers somewhat*: whatever Jephthah chooses—offer (O) or don't offer (Ō)—he prefers that God subsequently renege/relent (R).

		God		God			
		R	R̄	R/R	R̄/R̄	R/R̄	R̄/R
Jephthah	O	(4,3)	(2,4)	(4,3)	ⓐ(2,4)	(4,3)	(2,4)	⎱ Neither strategy dominant—
	Ō	(3,1)	(1,2)	(3,1)	(1̄,2)	(1,2)	(3,1)	⎰ must anticipate God's choice

↑
Don't renege/relent regardless dominant

c. *Jephthah wavers seriously*: same as (b) above, except given God is adamant (R̄), Jephthah prefers not to offer (Ō).

		God		God			
		R	R̄	R/R	R̄/R̄	R/R̄	R̄/R
Jephthah	O	(4,3)	(1,4)	(4,3)	(1̄,4)	(4,3)	(1,4)	⎱ Neither strategy dominant—
	Ō	(3,1)	(2,2)	(3,1)	ⓐ(2,2)	(2,2)	(3,1)	⎰ must anticipate God's choice

↑
Don't renege/relent regardless dominant

Key:
(x,y) = (Jephthah, God)
4 = best; 3 = next best; 2 = next worst; 1 = worst
Circled outcome rational

Figure 3.3 Payoff matrices for Jephthah's sacrifice: show-of-faith interpretation of God's preferences

come in which Jephthah offers and God accepts God's best (4) rather than His next-best (3), God's rational strategy choice is changed from conditional cooperation (tit-for-tat) to unconditional noncooperation (don't renege/relent regardless).

When Jephthah is faithful regardless under interpretation (a), he, like Abraham, has a dominant strategy of offering his child, obtaining his next-best outcome (3) when God accepts his offer. And like Abraham, Jephthah does worse if he wavers somewhat and God does not renege (2); to avoid his worst outcome of 1 under interpretation (b), he must anticipate God's dominant strategy choice, for he himself does not have one.

Thus, if faith does not sustain Jephthah, game-theoretic rationality will if he does not waver too seriously. Yet, if Jephthah wavers more—under interpretation (c)—his rational choice is *not* to offer his daughter. Neither God nor Jephthah will be happy with the resulting (2,2) outcome, however, especially since both could do better if they chose strategies associated with one of the (4,3) outcomes.

The problem with this game, like the famous Prisoners' Dilemma game, is that the rational choices of both players lead to an outcome [(2,2)] inferior for both players to

some other outcome(s) [(4,3)].[2] The better outcomes in the figure 3.3 (c) payoff matrix, however, are unstable: once either (4,3) outcome is chosen, God has an incentive to switch His strategy to $\overline{R}/\overline{R}$ or $\overline{R}/R$, which results in (1,4), His best outcome but Jephthah's worst. Hence, Jephthah would not choose strategy O in the first place.

This game differs from Prisoners' Dilemma, however, in that one player (God) but not both have dominant strategies. Jephthah, who does not have a dominant strategy, must therefore anticipate God's dominant strategy choice in order to avoid his worst outcome (1), which would result if he offered to sacrifice his daughter and God did not renege.

Yet Jephthah did not refuse to consummate his vow, so interpretation (c) does not provide an explanation of the actual choices of the players in this game. Interpretations (a) and (b) work, on the other hand, which means that Jephthah's sacrifice has both a "faith" and a "rationality" explanation when God prefers a show of faith—with sacrifice preferred to nonsacrifice. This show-of-faith interpretation of God's preferences would not work in Abraham's case, however, because God's rational strategy choice under all three interpretations in figure 3.3 is to be unrelenting regardless, which He of course was not when Isaac was about to be sacrificed.

If God is more vindictive, He does better when Jephthah wavers seriously, as shown under interpretation (c) in figure 3.4 [compare the circled outcome (2,3) in this figure with the circled outcome (2,2) in figure 3.3 for this interpretation]. Under the vindictive interpretation of God's preferences, I no longer assume He most prefers that Jephthah offer to sacrifice his child, as I did in the figure 3.3 (figure 3.2) interpretation. Instead, I assume that God most prefers not to renege/relent ($\overline{R}$), with his best outcome (4) occurring when Jephthah offers (O), his next-best outcome (3) when Jephthah does not offer ($\overline{O}$). Note that the only difference between the figure 3.3 and figure 3.4 games is that preference rankings "3" and "2" for God are interchanged in the payoff matrices.

As with the show-of-faith interpretation in figure 3.3, God always has a dominant strategy of being unrelenting regardless ($\overline{R}/\overline{R}$). A blindly faithful and somewhat wavering Jephthah will offer to sacrifice his daughter—confirming the choices reported in the Bible—but if Jephthah is somewhat wavering, he must first anticipate God's dominant strategy choice in order to make his own rational choice. As

with the show-of-faith interpretation of God's preferences, a seriously wavering Jephthah playing against a vindictive God would not offer to sacrifice his daughter, so interpretation (c) for both the show-of-faith and vindictive interpretations does not provide a rational explanation of the biblical outcome in this game.

In summary, a less merciful God than in Abraham's case must be posited to explain the choices of Jephthah and God in the game played over the sacrifice of Jephthah's daughter. It is not necessary, however, to assume God to be totally vindictive—that His two best outcomes are associated with the consummation of Jephthah's vow—in order to explain rationally the players' choices in this game. Indeed, the two months' respite granted Jephthah's daughter supports the proposition that God could tolerate some delay.

As with Abraham's sacrifice, both "faith" and "rationality" constitute alternative explanations of Jephthah's sacrifice. In Jephthah's case, however, the rationality explanation works only if Jephthah is somewhat wavering: he prefers to offer his daughter if God is adamant, otherwise not. Thus, while a sympathetic God allows a biblical character (Abraham) more free rein, even an unsympathetic God affords

a. *Jephthah faithful regardless*: whatever God chooses subsequently—renege/relent (R) or not (R̄)—Jephthah prefers to offer (O).

		God		God			
		R	R̄	R/R	R̄/R̄	R̄/R	R/R̄
Jephthah	O	(4,2)	(3,4)	(4,2)	⟨(3,4)⟩	(4,2)	(3,4)	← Offer dominant
	Ō	(2,1)	(1,3)	(2,1)	(1̄,3)	(1,3)	(2,1)

↑
Don't renege/relent regardless dominant

b. *Jephthah wavers somewhat*: whatever Jephthah chooses—offer (O) or don't offer (Ō)—he prefers that God subsequently renege/relent (R).

		God		God			
		R	R̄	R/R	R̄/R̄	R̄/R	R/R̄
Jephthah	O	(4,2)	(2,4)	(4,2)	⟨(2,4)⟩	(4,2)	(2,4)
	Ō	(3,1)	(1,3)	(3,1)	(1̄,3)	(1,3)	(3,1)

} Neither strategy dominant—must anticipate God's choice

↑
Don't renege/relent regardless dominant

c. *Jephthah wavers seriously*: same as (b) above, except given God is adamant (R̄), Don't renege/relent regardless dominant prefers not to offer (Ō).

		God		God			
		R	R̄	R/R	R̄/R̄	R̄/R	R/R̄
Jephthah	O	(4,2)	(1,4)	(4,2)	(1,4)	(4,2)	(1,4)
	Ō	(3,1)	(2,3)	(3,1)	⟨(2,3)⟩	(2,3)	(3,1)

} Neither strategy dominant—must anticipate God's choice

↑
Don't renege/relent regardless dominant

Key:
(x,y) = (Jephthah, God)
4 = best; 3 = next best; 2 = next worst; 1 = worst
Circled outcome rational

Figure 3.4 Payoff matrices for Jephthah's sacrifice: vindictive interpretation of God's preferences

a wavering character (Jephthah) the opportunity to make rational calculations that prevent his worst outcome from occurring.

3.4 Other Interpretations and Conclusions

It hardly needs to be pointed out that not all analysts see a calculating rationality at work in the biblical stories I have analyzed in this chapter. Kierkegaard, for example, in a stunningly prolix and self-conscious treatment of the Isaac story, argues that Abraham, having no authoritative basis on which to choose between obeying God or refusing to sacrifice his son's life, was stricken with dread that made his supreme act of faith all the more magnificent and courageous.[3] Kolakowski, on the other hand, disparages this interpretation and says that Abraham was simply following God's orders:

Superiors are not in the habit of explaining orders to subordinates. The essence of an order is that it must be executed because it is an order and not because it is reasonable, promising of success, or well thought out. It is by no means required that the executant understand its meaning; were it so, it would inevitably lead to anarchy and chaos. A subordinate who asks about the meaning of an order is a sower of disorder, a sterile argumentative person. At bottom, he is a smart aleck, an enemy of authority, of the social order, and of the Establishment.[4]

Kolakowski, in his usual irreverent way, goes on to embellish the Isaac story by adding that Abraham botched the sacrifice. After Isaac discovered his father's intent, Kolakowski insists, he "never got over his shock."[5]

Kierkegaard also offers a scenario in which Abraham does not conceal his intent.[6] Indeed, the Jewish commentator Rashi says unequivocally that when Abraham answered Isaac's question about the whereabouts of the sacrificial sheep by responding that "God will see to the sheep for His burnt offering, my son" (Gen. 22:8), Isaac understood he was to be murdered.[7]

If Isaac were aware of his impending fate, he might perhaps be included with Abraham and God as a player in a more complex three-person game. In my opinion, however, even if Isaac were aware of his intended sacrifice, the game is adequately—and more parsimoniously—modeled as one played between its two principal players, Abraham and God.

I would also argue that Jephthah's sacrifice was essentially a two-person game, though in this story there is no question that Jephthah's daughter was not only aware of her fate but, because of this, was also able to obtain a temporary reprieve. Yet her foreknowledge had no effect on the final outcome.

What light does game theory cast on the meaning of these stories of sacrifice in the Old Testament and the nature of their players? First, I believe, the game-theoretic interpretations I have offered provide plausible *alternative* explanations for the choices made by the human biblical characters, based on their own preferences and the perceived preferences of the other player, God. In particular, if Abraham and Jephthah were completely faithful servants of God, their own preferences suffice to direct their actions.[8] But if Abraham and Jephthah waver, they no longer have dominant strategies and must, instead, anticipate God's choice of a dominant strategy—based on His preferences—to act rationally themselves.

If God is sympathetic, as in Abraham's case, Abraham can waver seriously and still act rationally by offering his son. Some wavering is possible if God is less sympathetic, as in Jephthah's case, but if Jephthah prizes his daughter's life above everything else, it is not rational for him to offer to sacrifice her, given the two sets of preferences I have postulated for God,

and Jephthah's awareness of these. Since Jephthah did in fact consummate his vow, the game-theoretic analysis suggests he had greater faith in—or fear of—God.

As with Abraham, however, given the different human preferences I have postulated, it is impossible to ascertain whether biblical characters were blindly faithful or wavering. Thus, a major alternative explanation of their actions might be that they did indeed waver, but anticipating God's rational strategy, they were compelled by their own rationality to demonstrate their faith by offering to sacrifice their children. In one case the outcome was clearly salutary for the father, but in the other it was heartbreaking.

Even for Jephthah, however, this is not to say that his action was irrational. Rather, he seems to have been caught up in a truly gruesome game. Perhaps the story of Jephthah is "exceptional and cannot be treated as indicative of the norm of human sacrifice in Israel."[9] Nonetheless, if Jephthah had not made his parlous vow, he presumably would have been killed in battle with the Ammonites. Moreover, he not only lived for several years after the sacrifice but also won other military victories and ruled as judge (a political-military leader in biblical times) until his death. In the parallel

Greek legend related in Euripides's play, *Iphigenia in Aulis*, Agamemnon, too, (temporarily) survived the sacrifice of his daughter, Iphigenia.[10]

God, it appears from the stories I have analyzed, may be merciful, vindictive, or even ambivalent. Whatever his mood or preferences, however, it seems not beyond the pale to interpret His choices as if He were a player in a game. In fact, when confronted by a human player who is told, or gains some understanding of, His preferences, the conditions for modeling their choices in a game are met.

Most of the interpretations I have offered of God and His protagonists as rational actors are consistent with the outcomes of the stories of sacrifice I have analyzed. Only when Jephthah wavers seriously does game theory predict an outcome different from that which occurred, whether God's preferences are viewed as show-of-faith or vindictive. This means that a seriously wavering Jephthah must be rejected, but not necessarily a seriously wavering Abraham, given the preferences of God I have postulated and the awareness of these by God's human protagonists. In either case, both biblical characters need not be blindly faithful to explain the choices they made under extremely difficult personal circumstances. This fact—that faith is not

necessarily the engine that drives these characters—provides, I believe, an alternative explanation for the outcomes of these games.

That God's mood changes from one story to the other makes Him appear inconsistent—forgiving and sympathetic on one occasion, angry and vindictive on another. If God does not always appear cool and even-tempered, however, I submit this has no bearing on His rationality. The question is, *given* His moods and preferences—however erratic they may appear—do He and His protagonists make choices consistent with their preferences in a game?

The evidence from the two stories I have analyzed, backed up by both "faith" and "rationality" arguments, is that they do. The difference between these arguments, however, is that faith, though rational, is not game theoretic in the calculating sense: a faithful character, by virtue of having a dominant strategy, need not consider what other players do but need only consult his own preferences. Whether faith expresses a character's trust in, or fear of, God, it allows him to act blindly, thereby lifting from him the burden of sophisticated calculations. But we cannot be sure that the fathers in the two stories analyzed here did not make precisely these calculations.

Family Conflict

4.1 Introduction

There is probably no more excruciating test of a biblical character's faith than making his affirmation of God conditional on his sacrifice of a child. It is an unbearable choice for a parent, but when forced to choose, Abraham and Jephthah were ready to make that choice. As I have shown, however, their affirmations may have been rooted to a rationality other than blind faith.

Although it was Abraham and Jephthah's children who made the conflicts in their stories so poignant, these conflicts were not really family conflicts. Rather, the fathers' conflicts were with God, the instigator of many but certainly not all conflicts in biblical games.

All the stories I shall analyze in this chapter are from Genesis, and all involve conflicts between brothers. But that is about their only similarity. The first conflict I shall discuss, between Cain and Abel, leads to fratricide, but the game the murderer plays is not with his victim but, as in several previous stories, with God. However, the conflict that gives rise to this game, though inspired by God, occurs within the family, and for this reason I consider it a family conflict. This was not the case in the two sacrifice stories discussed in chapter 3: the interests of the fathers did not clash with those of their children, putting aside the demands made by God.

In the other two stories, God's role is much less prominent. The conflict between Esau and Jacob has two parts, the first involving just the two brothers, the second bringing in the parents. The conflict between Joseph and his brothers also involves the father, Jacob, but it is mainly a story of betrayal and deception by the brothers of each other.

I have focused on family conflict in this chapter not only because of its prominence in the Old Testament but also because of its immediacy—it hits home, literally and figuratively. The conflicts in our own families may not reach the intensity that led to the murder of Abel or the abandonment of Joseph, but there is no denying that conflicts within families have a powerful emotional impact on their members' lives. The question I want to examine is whether this emotion-laden conflict, at least in the Bible, has a rational basis as well.

4.2 Cain and Abel

After being driven from the garden of Eden, Adam and Eve became parents first to Cain and then to Abel. Cain was a tiller of the soil; Abel, a shepherd. As if incapable of letting things take their own course after the expulsion of Adam and Eve from the garden of Eden, God set up the conditions for conflict once again:

In the course of time, Cain brought an offering to the LORD from the fruit of the soil; and Abel, for his part, brought the choicest of the firstlings of his flock. The LORD paid heed to Abel and his offering, but to Cain and his offering He paid no heed. Cain was much distressed and his face fell. (Gen. 4:3–5)

Unlike the constraint game between Adam, Eve, and God discussed in section 2.4, this time God does not place limits on human choice and wait for them to be violated; He meddles directly in the affairs of the brothers by playing favorites, naturally antagonizing the one not favored.

True, Cain's offering was apparently inferior to Abel's, because it was simply from the "fruit of the soil" (Gen. 4:3) but not, like Abel's, the "choicest" (Gen. 4:4). Yet, if God was disappointed by its meagerness, why did He not say so, instead of paying no heed to Cain? God had not been silent about His distress with Adam and Eve's transgressions.

In fact, I believe, God's primary motive was less to chastise Cain than to alleviate His boredom by stirring up jealousy between the brothers—and then await the fireworks. If this was His goal, He was not to be disappointed.

As support for this position, consider God's incredible question after refusing Cain's offering and observing his anger:

Why are you distressed,
And why is your face fallen? (Gen. 4:6)

Without awaiting an answer, which I presume God knew and did not want to respond to, God offered His own version of poetic justice likely to befall recalcitrants like Cain:

Surely, if you do right,
There is uplift.
But if you do not do right
Sin couches at the door;
Its urge is toward you,
Yet you can be its master. (Gen. 4:7)

Having issued this warning, God immediately observed the divine consequences of His provocation of Cain:

Cain said to his brother Abel [Ancient versions: "Come, let us go into the field"] . . . and when they were in the field, Cain set upon his brother Abel and killed him. (Gen. 4:8)

Next comes another incredible question from God, reminiscent of the rhetorical question He asked Adam about his whereabouts after Adam ate the forbidden fruit (section 2.6): "Where is your brother Abel?" (Gen. 4:9). Cain's memorable response is less than forthcoming: "I do not know. Am I my brother's keeper?" (Gen. 4:9).

This acerbic answer in the form of a question, I submit, gives us as much insight into Cain's strategic calculations as it does into his shaky morality. First, there seems little doubt that his murder of Abel was premeditated, for he set upon Abel "in the field" (Gen. 4:8), to which, it seems, they journeyed together.[1] Second, warned by God of the presence of sin at his door, Cain cannot be excused for being unaware that his crime might have adverse consequences, even if their exact nature could not be foreseen.

Seething with anger and jealousy over the favoritism shown Abel, and unable to strike out against God directly (even if he had wanted to), Cain did the next best thing—he murdered God's apparent favorite. Under the circumstances, this response to God's taunting from a terribly aggrieved man seems to me not at all irrational.

What is harder to understand is Cain's reply about being his brother's keeper. In my opinion, it can be read as a cleverly constructed challenge to God's own morality in meddling in the affairs of the brothers.[2] Not that Cain necessarily knew that God had fomented trouble to test Cain's susceptibility to sin—or simply to roil the waters. Whoever was to blame, however, Cain felt deeply wronged and was driven to take revenge.

But how does one justify fratricide, and what can one do after the act to mitigate one's punishment for the crime? Cain had at least three courses of action open to him:

1. Admit the murder.
2. Deny the murder.
3. Defend his morality.

Admittedly, the third course of action would seem hard to execute shamelessly, except when it is recalled that the conditions that led to the crime do not leave God with virtuous intent intact.

Whether one perfidy justifies another, the salient fact is that Cain did not think his act unjustified. Even if he had no suspicion of God's less-than-virtuous intent, he could still perhaps defend himself by pleading no responsibility for his brother's welfare.

Cain's defense is actually more subtle than simply a plea of inculpability. He first says he does not know where his brother is. Could not this imply that God does or should know, and that He bears some responsibility for Abel, too? The notion that Abel is not Cain's sole responsibility is then reinforced by Cain's famous question.

This, in my opinion, is a brilliant defense, because it eloquently contrasts God's responsibility and his own, implicitly suggesting that there may be questionable morality on both sides. God, in His response to Cain's (unadmitted) crime and rhetorical defense, begins with His own rhetorical question, which He quickly follows with a stiff sentence for a tiller of the soil:

What have you done? Hark, your brother's blood cries out to me from the ground! Therefore, you shall be more cursed than the ground, which opened its mouth to receive your brother's blood from your hand. If you till the soil, it shall no longer yield its strength to you. You shall become a ceaseless wanderer on earth. (Gen. 4:10–12)

Acting as his own defense attorney, Cain responded to God's sentence with a plea for mercy:

My punishment is too great to bear! Since You have banished me this day from the soil, and I must avoid Your presence and become a restless wanderer on earth—anyone who meets me may kill me! (Gen. 4:13–14)

Note that the crux of Cain's plaintive remonstration is that he might be killed, not that the sentence itself is unjust or inappropriate. Reminded of this consequence of His sentence, God finds it unpalatable and answers Cain by saying:

"I promise, if anyone kills Cain, sevenfold vengeance shall be taken on him." And the LORD put a mark on Cain, lest anyone who met him should kill him. (Gen. 4:15)

The reason, I believe, God finds Cain's death unpalatable is because only "a ceaseless wanderer on earth" (Gen. 4:12) can spread far and wide the message of God's retribution for fratricide. If Cain were quickly dispatched, God's great power—and even greater mercy in sparing the murderer's life—would of course not get communicated to the world.

I postulate that God considered two strategies in response to Cain's murder of Abel:

1. Kill Cain.
2. Punish Cain.

If Cain had either admitted his crime or denied it, I believe God would probably have chosen to kill Cain. Murder, especially of one's brother, is too serious a crime to ignore or cover up. Moreover, the execution of the murderer would set an impressive precedent.

If there were extenuating circumstances, on the other hand, punishment short of death could be considered. Yet there was no serpent, as in the Adam and Eve story (section 2.5), that could be implicated and used as exculpation for Cain's sin. The only possible extenuating circumstance was God's complicity—or at least His failure to accept any responsibility for bestirring trouble in the first place, or for not coming to Abel's aid just before his murder.

This failure, and perhaps the resulting guilt God felt, is exactly what Cain's reply to God plays upon. It is as if Cain said, "He's your responsibility, too; why did you not protect him from my rage, which after all you incited?" If God is not disturbed by this implied question, why would He say that Abel's blood "cries out *to Me* from the ground" (Gen. 4:10; my italics)—not to Cain, not to the world, but to God Himself. God is responsible, too.[3]

God can hardly condemn a man to death when He is also culpable. Consequently, He only banishes Cain from the ground where his brother's blood was shed and spares his life. In fact, Cain, as I have already indicated, is able to extract still more from a now troubled God: a mark that signals to anyone meeting him that he should not be killed. Would an untroubled God be so attentive to the pleas of a murderer whom He had previously warned? Coupled with God's desire to promulgate to the world both His power and mercy, a commutation of Cain's sentence seems sensible for God.

My exegesis of the Cain and Abel story in rational-choice terms is summarized as a game played between Cain and God in figure 4.1. Very briefly, working backward from the bottom of the tree, I would rate all outcomes as "medium" or "bad" for God except that of punishing Cain after he mounts a defense of his morality that indirectly implicates God. Even if this defense creates guilt or shame in God, on balance, I believe, He would prefer to act mercifully (if given good reasons) than to act too harshly by killing Cain—"medium" outcomes in figure 4.1—or too benevolently by sparing him (without good reasons)—"bad" outcomes. (These "medium" and "bad" outcomes for God at the bottom of the tree could be reversed without changing the results of the analysis.) In addition, an alive Cain wandering the earth can tell the world that God punished him but mercifully spared his life. This will be good for God's image—and salve His disquieting feelings about the episode.

Proceeding up the tree, Cain would prefer an outcome that God regards as "good," and he as "medium," to being killed for simply admitting or denying his crime ("bad" for Cain, "medium" for

God). In turn, Cain should murder Abel—rather than feeling self-pity in not avenging his humiliation—for this "bad" outcome is inferior to the "medium" outcome resulting from Abel's murder, Cain's defense, and God's punishment. At the top of the tree, it is clearly rational for God, anticipating future rational choices, to incite jealousy between the brothers—with ultimate "good" consequences for the image He wants to create—rather than to do nothing and be rather bored with Himself after the excitement with Adam, Eve, and the serpent had subsided.

Both the origin and resolution of the family conflict between Cain and Abel are obviously affected by the heavy hand of God. Indeed, I do not consider Abel even to be a player, capable of making choices, in my game-theoretic treatment of his murder and its consequences. In the next family conflict, God's hand is less heavy, but in His place sits a father whose presence introduces generational conflict into what seems at first simple sibling rivalry

4.3 Jacob and Esau

Isaac, it will be recalled (section 3.2), was the son of Abraham. His wife, Rebekah, was barren, and Isaac appealed to God on her behalf. She conceived and carried twins, who pressed hard against

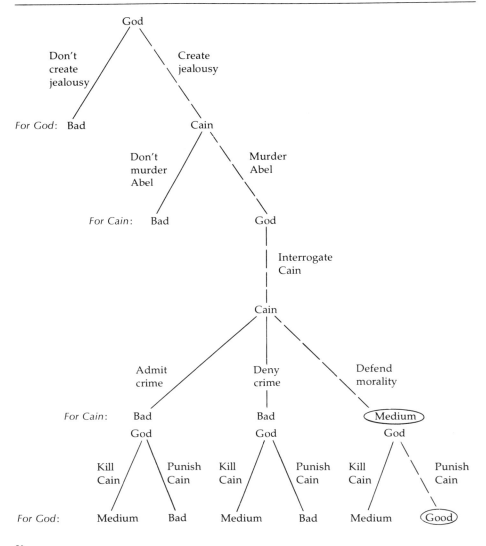

Key:
Rational choices for Cain and God circled

Figure 4.1 Game tree of Cain's murder of Abel

each other in her womb. Taking this to be an omen, Rebekah asked God what it meant. He replied:

Two nations are in your womb,
Two separate peoples shall issue from your body;
One people shall be mightier than the other,
And the older shall serve the younger. (Gen. 25:23)

This cryptic interpretation foreshadows the future relationship between the twins and the games they were to play in later encounters.

The Bible offers a vivid account of the twins' birth, and then describes their development:

The first one emerged red, like a hairy mantle all over; so they named him Esau. Then his brother emerged, holding on to the heel of Esau; so they named him Jacob. (Gen. 25:25-26)

The beginnings of family conflict that transcend sibling rivalry are prefigured in the next passage:

Isaac favored Esau because he had a taste for game; but Rebekah favored Jacob. (Gen. 25:28)

The first conflict to arise between the brothers does not include their parents:

Once when Jacob was cooking a stew, Esau came in from the open, famished. And Esau said to Jacob, "Give me some of that red stuff to gulp down, for I am famished"—which is why he was named Edom [Red]. Jacob said, "First sell me your birthright." And Esau said, "I am at the point of death, so of what use is my birthright to me?" But Jacob said, "Swear to me first." So he swore to him, and sold his birthright to Jacob. Jacob then gave Esau bread and lentil stew; he ate and drank, and he rose and went away. Thus did Esau spurn the birthright. (Gen. 25:29-34)

This conflict can be described by the outcome matrix shown in figure 4.2. Esau can either sell his birthright or not; Jacob can either give or not give him food. The outcomes that result from these strategy choices, with player rankings, are:

Transaction completed (3,4): Esau sells his birthright for the food, obtaining his next-best outcome; Jacob keeps his promise and gives Esau the food, obtaining his best outcome.

Esau refuses, Jacob capitulates (4,1): the best outcome for Esau because he both faces down Jacob and receives food; the worst outcome for Jacob because his threat fails.

Jacob reneges, Esau dies (1,3): the worst outcome for Esau because, after complying with Jacob's threat, he receives no food and presumably dies; the next-best outcome for Jacob because he obtains the birth-

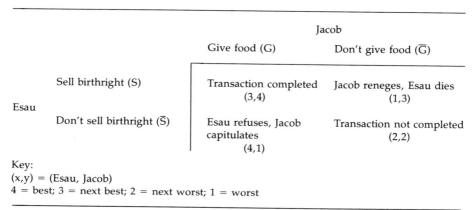

Figure 4.2 Outcome matrix of birthright game

right but then reneges on his promise without good reason.

Transaction not completed (2,2): the next-worst outcome for both players, because neither receives what he most desires; however, Jacob does not capitulate, and Esau keeps his birthright. Although Esau will presumably die, he will do so with his pride intact, while Jacob, even if he inherits the birthright, will be stricken with guilt.

Since Esau had the first move after Jacob announced his terms, the game is properly modeled as a 2 × 4 game, whose payoff matrix is shown in figure 4.3. Esau does not have a dominant strategy, but anticipating Jacob's choice of his dominant strategy of tit-for-tat, he would choose to sell his birthright, for "3" is better than "2" for him in

Jacob's tit-for-tat column. Thereby the transaction is completed as the Bible reports, and Jacob "wins."

The biblical comment, "Thus did Esau spurn the birthright" (Gen. 25:34), suggests that Esau "lost" this game. I reject this interpretation, however, because the game was not one of total conflict: both players would have lost if the transaction had not been completed. Saving his life by eating the food was certainly preferable for Esau to dying, which presumably would have been the outcome if he had refused to sell his birthright and Jacob, following tit-for-tat, had then given him no food. The value of Esau's birthright to Jacob is not entirely clear at this point, though obtaining it was essentially costless to him in the game just described. It directly bears on another right of

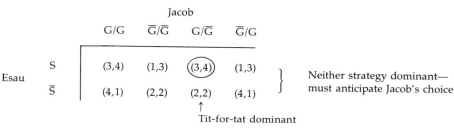

Jacob

	G/G	G̅/G̅	G/G̅	G̅/G
Esau S	(3,4)	(1,3)	((3,4))	(1,3)
Esau S̅	(4,1)	(2,2)	(2,2)	(4,1)

} Neither strategy dominant—must anticipate Jacob's choice

↑
Tit-for-tat dominant

Key:
(x,y) = (Esau, Jacob)
4 = best; 3 = next best; 2 = next worst; 1 = worst
Circled outcome rational

Figure 4.3 Payoff matrix of birthright game

the firstborn that is sought by both brothers in the next conflict to arise between them.

This conflict occurred after Esau married a Hittite, about whom Isaac and Rebekah felt "bitterness" (Gen. 26:35). Nonetheless, Isaac, old and no longer able to see, still wanted to give Esau his blessing before he died, and so told him. When Rebekah overheard this conversation, she used a ruse to make Jacob appear to be Esau so that he instead could obtain his father's blessing:

She covered his hands and the hairless part of his neck with the skins of the kids. Then she put in the hands of her son Jacob the dish and the bread that she had prepared.

He went to his father and said, "Father." And he said, "Yes, which of my sons are you?" Jacob said to his father, "I am Esau, your first-born; I have done as you told me. Pray sit up and eat of my game, that you may give your innermost blessing." (Gen. 27:16–19)

Isaac, not completely trusting what he heard, tested "Esau" (Jacob):

Come closer that I may feel you, my son—whether you are really my son Esau or not. (Gen. 27:21)

The results of the test were equivocal, but in the end Isaac blessed "Esau" (Jacob):

"The voice is the voice of Jacob, yet the hands are the hands of Esau." He did not recognize him, because his hands were hairy like those of his brother Esau; and so he blessed him.

He asked, "Are you really my son

Esau?'' And when he said, ''I am,'' he said, ''Serve me and let me eat of my son's game that I may give you my innermost blessing.'' (Gen. 27:22-25)

Jacob's blatant lie about his identity did not go long undiscovered. Scarcely after Jacob had left, Esau returned and also sought his father's blessing. Realizing that he had been deceived, Isaac ''was seized with very violent trembling'' (Gen. 27:33), and Esau ''burst into wild and bitter sobbing'' (Gen. 27:34), saying:

''Bless me too, Father!'' But he answered, ''Your brother came with guile and took away your blessing.'' [Esau] said, ''Was he, then, named Jacob that he might supplant me these two times? First he took away my birthright and now he has taken away my blessing!'' And he added, ''Have you not reserved any blessing for me?'' Isaac answered, saying to Esau, ''But I have made him master over you: I have given him all his brothers for servants, and sustained him with grain and wine. What, then, can I still do for you, my son?'' And Esau said to his father, ''Have you but one blessing, Father? Bless me too, Father!'' (Gen. 27:34-38)

But a blessing once uttered cannot be revoked and applied to another, so Esau thirsted for revenge. Rebekah once again came to Jacob's aid, helping him slip away to her brother Laban in Haran.

It is not easy to understand why Isaac, despite his apparent doubts about ''Esau's'' identity, still went ahead and blessed him. The best explanation I can offer is that he prized Esau mostly for his hunting and culinary skills, evidenced by the statement he made to Esau after announcing that his death was impending:

Take your gear, your quiver and bow, and go out into the open and hunt me some game. Then prepare a dish for me such as I like, and bring it to me to eat, so that I may give you my innermost blessing before I die. (Gen. 27:3-4)

This view of Isaac's attraction to Esau is underscored by Isaac's exclamation after smelling ''Esau's'' clothes:

Ah, the smell of my son is like the smell of the fields that the LORD has blessed. (Gen. 27:27)

For a father who puts so much emphasis on the outdoor life and gustatory pleasures, it is perhaps not all that surprising that when they are at hand, they would extirpate his misgivings about blessing a son who emits confusing signals.

It should also not be forgotten that Isaac was bitter about Esau's marriage to a Hittite. Even after his deception by Jacob, Isaac was still willing to instruct Jacob not to "take a wife from among the Canaanite [Hittite] women" (Gen. 28:1).

If Isaac's affection for Esau did not run deep, the same cannot be said for Rebekah's concern for Jacob. She did everything in her power to elevate Jacob's position above Esau's, first instigating his deception of her husband and then helping him make good his escape. To be sure, Jacob was not an unwilling accomplice, but Rebekah was the significant player behind the scenes.

The reasons underlying Rebekah's actions are hardest to discern. She favored Jacob, but why? The Bible is silent on this question. One may presume, of course, that Esau's masculinity was not as endearing to his mother as Jacob's more feminine qualities.

Neither was Rebekah enamored of Hittite women:

I am disgusted with my life because of the Hittite women. If Jacob marries a Hittite woman like these, from among the native women, what good will life be to me? (Gen. 27:46)

Rather strong stuff for a mother's feelings about a potential daughter-in-law!

Despite her greater attraction to Jacob, Rebekah was not uncon-cerned about Esau. Probably the most interesting strategic calculation in the entire story can be gleaned from Rebekah's revealing advice to Jacob as she prepared him for his escape:

Stay with him [Laban] a while, until your brother's fury subsides—until your brother's anger against you subsides—and he forgets what you have done to him. Then I will fetch you from there. Let me not lose you both in one day! (Gen. 27:44-45)

Indeed, Rebekah can have the best of all worlds if she helps to ensure Jacob's escape after he has received the blessing reserved for the first-born, makes it unlikely that he will marry a Hittite, and keeps Esau bottled up during a waiting period in which he will remain nonviolent while his anger subsides. Thus, Rebekah is engaged in a complex and subtle game involving her sons, her husband indirectly, and her future daughter-in-law. I will not try formally to model her calculations, for her "game" is really only a one-person affair involving first the deception of Isaac, then the spiriting away of Jacob.

That Rebekah is the consummate game player is confirmed by what later transpired. Jacob made good his escape, came upon his uncle Laban, and after a series of misadventures with Laban's two daughters, eventually married the one he loved. Most astounding, though, was his eventual reunion with Esau:

Looking up, Jacob saw Esau coming, accompanied by four hundred men. . . . [Jacob] bowed low to the ground seven times until he was near his brother. Esau ran to greet him. He embraced him, and, falling on his neck, he kissed him; and they wept. (Gen. 33:1–4)

An auspicious ending, indeed!

Jacob, the active player in the first conflict with Esau and the passive player in the second conflict, succeeded admirably in attaining the entitlements of the firstborn: birthright and his father's blessing. Esau bore no grudge in the end, for reasons that are less than clear. The best guess I can make is that he had a mercurial temperament—as his mother implied when she said his anger would subside after a while— which would make him quick to forget the wrongs done to him. Family loyalty, and indirectly obedience to God and His laws intended to preserve the family, may also have played a role.

God, it seems, quite well foresaw the struggle between the brothers, symbolized in the beginning by their exertions against each other in their mother's womb. But after prefiguring their conflict and its outcome, God did not enter the picture, as He did in pressing Cain for the truth about his brother's murder and then stigmatizing him. Rather, it was the brothers' mother, Rebekah, who played the significant behind-the-scenes role in the second conflict between Esau and Jacob and—almost godlike—manipulated events so as to enhance the position of her favorite, Jacob. In the final family conflict I shall analyze, intrigue swirls around Jacob's son, Joseph.

4.4 Joseph and His Brothers

Family conflict between sisters is not unheard of in the Bible, such as that which enveloped Jacob and both of Laban's daughters, the weak-eyed Leah and the beautiful and shapely Rachel, both of whom vied for Jacob's affection and his hand in marriage. But much more common is the kind of conflict described in chapter 3, in which parents anguish over their children, or the conflict between brothers in this chapter, with God on occasion playing the role of an antagonist testing a player (Abraham), holding him to his vow (Jephthah), or punishing him (Cain). Variations on these themes will be explored in future chapters.

The family conflict I shall next analyze again involves brothers. But this time it encompasses more than two, as well as a father who complicates the usual bilateral kind of relationship discussed in most of the previous stories.

As in the Cain and Abel story, the basic sibling conflict is fueled by the favoritism shown one brother in a family. Now, however, it is not God but Jacob—since renamed Israel because he had "striven with beings divine and human" (Gen. 32:29)—who sparks the jealousy:

Now Israel loved Joseph best of all his sons, for he was the child of his old age; and he had made him an ornamented tunic. And when his brothers saw that their father loved him more than any of his brothers, they hated him so that they could not speak a friendly word to him. (Gen. 37:3–4)

Joseph then had two dreams, both of which signified that he would come to rule over other members of his family, who would bow low before him. This enraged his ten older brothers even more, who plotted to kill him:

They said to one another, "Here comes that dreamer! Come now, let us kill him and throw him into one of the pits; and we can say, 'A savage beast devoured him.' We shall see what comes of his dreams!" (Gen. 37:19–20)

But one of his brothers, Reuben, interceded on Joseph's behalf:

When Reuben heard it, he tried to save him from them. He said, "Let us not take his life." And Reuben went on, "Shed no blood! Cast him into that pit out in the wilderness, but do not touch him yourselves." (Gen. 37:21–22)

After the brothers stripped Joseph of his ornamented tunic, he was thrown into the pit.

But Joseph was rescued by traders who chanced by, who in turn sold him to Ishmaelites on their way to Egypt. Meanwhile, to hide their betrayal of Joseph, the brothers devised a clever cover-up:

They took Joseph's tunic, slaughtered a kid, and dipped the tunic in the blood. They had the ornamented tunic taken to their father, and they said, "We found this. Please examine it; is it your son's tunic or not?" He recognized it, and said, "My son's tunic! A savage beast devoured him! Joseph was torn by a beast!" (Gen. 37:31–33)

Grief-stricken, Jacob vowed to "go down mourning to my son in Sheol [the underworld]" (Gen. 37:35).

But Joseph, of course, was very much alive. After the Ishmaelites brought him to Egypt, they sold him to Potiphar, Pharaoh's chief steward. The Bible reports that "the LORD was with Joseph, and he was a successful man" (Gen. 39:2).

After being falsely accused of seducing Potiphar's wife, however, Joseph was imprisoned. In prison he successfully interpreted dreams of Pharaoh's chief cupbearer and baker and then was called upon to interpret two dreams of Pharaoh. His interpretation—that there would be seven years of plenty followed by seven years of famine—so impressed Pharaoh that he put Joseph in charge of building up grain reserves so that the country would be able to withstand the predicted famine. When it in fact occurred, and its devastating impact was felt, "all the world came to Joseph in Egypt to procure rations, for the famine had become severe throughout the world" (Gen. 41:57).

The reunion of the brothers is prepared for when Jacob asks his sons to procure rations in Egypt to avert their starvation in Canaan. He insists, however, that Benjamin, his youngest son, stay behind "since he feared that he might meet with disaster" (Gen. 42:4).

Joseph's brothers journeyed to Egypt and met Joseph, who, as vizier of the land, "dispensed rations to all the people of the land" (Gen. 42:6):

Joseph's brothers came and bowed low to him, with their faces to the ground. When Joseph saw his brothers, he recognized them; but he acted like a stranger toward them and spoke harshly to them. He asked them, "Where do you come from?" And they said, "From the land of Canaan, to procure food." For though Joseph recognized his brothers, they did not recognize him. Recalling the dreams that he had dreamed about them, Joseph said to them, "You are spies, you have come to see the land in its nakedness." (Gen. 42:6-9)

The brothers protested their innocence, but to no avail. Finally, after learning from the brothers about Benjamin's retention in Canaan with his father, Joseph said that he would test them:

By this you shall be put to the test: unless your youngest brother comes here, by Pharaoh, you shall not depart from this place! Let one of you go and bring your brother, while the rest of you remain confined, that your words may be put to the test whether there is truth in you. Else, by Pharaoh, you are nothing but spies! (Gen. 42:15-16)

Insisting that he was a "God-fearing man" (Gen. 42:18), Joseph then relaxed his demand and said that he would keep only one brother as hostage:

If you are honest men, let one of you brothers be held in your place of detention, while the rest of you go and take home rations for your starving households; but you must bring me your youngest brother, that your words may be verified and that you may not die. (Gen. 42:19–20)

The brothers felt guilty and said to one another:

Alas, we are being punished on account of our brother [Joseph], because we looked on at his anguish, yet paid no heed as he pleaded with us. That is why this distress has come upon us. (Gen. 42:21)

In any event, Simeon was the brother left behind as hostage, but Joseph played a trick on the returning brothers: he not only had their bags filled with grain but also saw to it that the money they had brought him as payment for the grain was returned to their sacks:

Their hearts sank; and, trembling, they turned to one another, saying, "What is this that God has done to us?" (Gen. 42:28)

Jacob was indignant with his sons after they reported the results of their journey:

It is always me that you bereave: Joseph is no more and Simeon is no more, and now you would take away

Benjamin. These things always happen to me! (Gen. 42:36)

A debate then ensued between Jacob and his sons about whether to return with Benjamin. Judah's argument to his father, in particular, rang with a hard-headed realism:

The man [Joseph] warned us, "Do not let me see your faces unless your brother [Benjamin] is with you." If you will let our brother go with us, we will go down and procure food for you; but if you will not let him go, we will not go down, for the man said to us, "Do not let me see your faces unless your brother is with you." (Gen. 43:3–5)

Later, in exasperation, Judah added:

Send the boy in my care, and let us be on our way, that we may live and not die—you and we and our children. I myself will be surety for him; you may hold me responsible: if I do not bring him back to you and set him before you, I shall stand guilty before you forever. For we could have been there and back twice if we had not dawdled. (Gen. 43:8–10)

To reinforce the claim that the brothers would not simply abandon Benjamin (as Jacob might have suspected they did Joseph earlier), another brother, Reuben, who had earlier saved Joseph from death by interceding before his brothers, promised his father that he would kill both his sons if he did not return with Benjamin. In the end Jacob relented, and Benjamin returned with his brothers to Egypt.

As I see the strategic situation, Jacob and his sons, whom I model as two players because of their internal differences, had three options. The brothers could

1. Return with Benjamin.
2. Return without Benjamin.
3. Not return.

In response to option 1, Joseph could either

1. Hold Benjamin.
2. Let Benjamin return.

These sequential choices, and a description and ranking of the resulting outcomes, are shown in the game tree in figure 4.4.

To analyze this tree, first note that Jacob and his sons fundamentally disagree about three of the four possible outcomes. Putting aside the (4,4,4) outcome—best for all three players (Jacob, sons, Joseph)—consider the three other outcomes in this n-person game:

(3,1,1) What is next best for Jacob (3) is worst for his sons (1): Jacob starves, but he does so in the com-

pany of Benjamin; the other sons all die.

(1,3,3) What is next best for the sons (3) is worst for Jacob (1): the sons' fate is uncertain; Jacob dies forlorn without Benjamin.

(2,2,2) Next worst for both Jacob and sons (2): Jacob starves in the company of Benjamin, but his other sons are imprisoned; their imprisonment is better than starvation but worse than their uncertain fate should Joseph hold Benjamin.

If Joseph held Benjamin, the brothers might feel terribly guilty about having failed their father, but I believe they perceived leaving Benjamin behind to be still less satisfactory. True, Joseph was vague about the consequences of their disregarding his order to return with Benjamin, saying only, "Do not let me see your faces" (Gen. 44:23). But this threat seemed to imply their imprisonment at the least, and possibly their execution.

Even if the brothers were ignorant of the (4,4,4) outcome, they would prefer to return with Benjamin (3) than not return (1) or return without him (2). Although Jacob had the opposite preferences—at least initially—the sons' choice was decisive, and in the end they seem to have succeeded in persuading their anxious father of the logic of their assessment.

Although Joseph made no choice

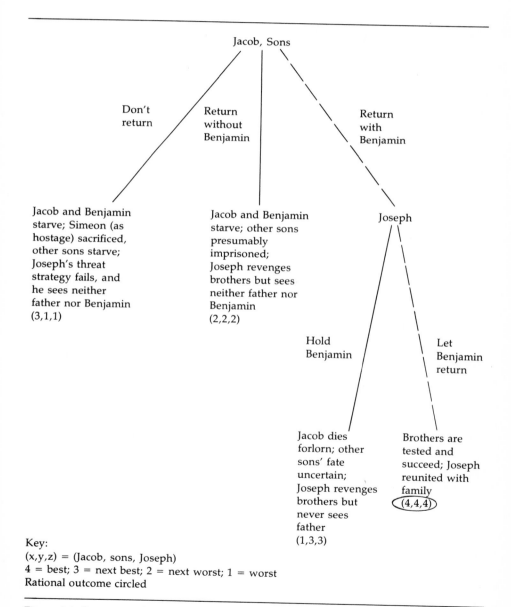

Key:
(x,y,z) = (Jacob, sons, Joseph)
4 = best; 3 = next best; 2 = next worst; 1 = worst
Rational outcome circled

Figure 4.4 Game tree of Joseph's threat

with respect to Benjamin's return, he preferred that his threat not be a total failure (1: if the brothers did not return) but a partial failure (2: if they returned without Benjamin). In the latter case, Joseph at least could take revenge on his brothers, not just the single hostage, Simeon—though he may never have intended to kill any of his brothers, since they had allowed him to live earlier.

What seemed to disturb Jacob most was dying alone in Canaan, without Benjamin at his side, especially since his former favorite, Joseph, had been lost. Yet perhaps he foresaw, however dimly, that the family might be reunited in Canaan and not starve, unequivocally the best outcome for all players [(4,4,4)] after Joseph revealed his identity.

Not knowing Joseph's true identity, though, it is hard for the brothers to predict what he will do with Benjamin. But since he said he was a God-fearing man, and since Judah was willing to go as surety for Benjamin, and Reuben to kill his sons should the brothers not return with Benjamin, the balance is tipped in favor of taking Joseph's word at face value. Thus, even though the brothers do not see through to Joseph's true motives and interests in this situation, Judah's argument that returning with Benjamin will

save everybody—"you and we and our children" (Gen. 43:8)—makes the brothers' case against their father finally compelling.

The game, in other words, is played *as if* the rankings I have assumed in figure 4.4 were known. The preponderance of evidence available to the brothers favored Joseph's preferring to let Benjamin return. What was least discernible to them was that this would turn out to be their best outcome, too, since they did not know that Joseph was their long-lost brother and that the family would be reunited. But again the brothers sensed, I believe, that returning without Benjamin could be disastrous for them, so they were willing in the end to take the calculated risk that Joseph would remain true to his word. Given this presumption, they should return with Benjamin, and Joseph in turn would (they hoped) do what he had promised.

What actually occurred after the brothers returned with Benjamin created further discomfort for them. Recalling the money that they found in their bags, the brothers entered Joseph's house with trepidation, bringing Benjamin. Joseph, however, immediately disabused them of their fears:

All is well with you; do not be afraid. Your God and the God of your father must have put treasure in your bags for you. I got your payment. (Gen. 43:23)

Thus was one snag removed.

Upon seeing his youngest brother Benjamin, who had not been born when his other brothers had cast him into the pit, Joseph almost broke down but managed to control himself. After composing himself in another room, Joseph returned and could not resist testing the brothers once again: this time he not only ordered that the brothers' money be returned to their bags, but he also directed his steward to place his own silver goblet in Benjamin's bag.

A new round of extortion then commenced. Shortly after the brothers departed, Joseph ordered his steward to overtake the brothers and say:

Why did you repay good with evil? It [the silver goblet] is the very one from which my master drinks and which he uses for divination. It was a wicked thing for you to do! (Gen. 44:4–5)

After this denunciation, the brothers were nonplussed. Disbelieving, they replied:

Whichever of your servants it is found with shall die; the rest of us, moreover, shall become slaves to my lord. (Gen. 44:9)

The steward, however, demanded less:

Only the one with whom it is found shall be my slave; but the rest of you shall go free. (Gen. 44:10)

When the goblet was found in Benjamin's bag, the brothers were thunderstruck; they returned to Joseph's house and beseeched him not to hold Benjamin. Judah told Joseph about their father's great love for his youngest son—having already lost Benjamin's only full brother (Joseph; the other brothers were not Rachel's children)—and that he would surely die in despair if Benjamin were not returned. Saying that he went as surety for Benjamin, Judah made the following proposal in his peroration:

Please let your servant remain as a slave to my lord instead of the boy, and let the boy go back with his brothers. For how can I go back to my father unless the boy is with me? Let me not be witness to the woe that would overtake my father! (Gen. 44:33–34)

Deeply moved and unable to control himself any longer, Joseph ordered his attendants to leave. Weeping loudly, he revealed himself to his brothers, at the same time absolving them of responsibility for their earlier betrayal of him:

"I am Joseph. Is my father still well?" But his brothers could not answer him, so dumbfounded were they on account of him.

Then Joseph said to his brothers, "Come forward to me." And when they came forward, he said, "I am your brother Joseph, he whom you sold into Egypt. Now, do not be distressed or reproach yourselves because you sold me hither; it was to save life that God sent me ahead of you." (Gen. 45:3-5)

In a final emotional scene, Joseph, not without a touch of boastfulness, said:

"And you must tell my father everything about my high station in Egypt and all that you have seen; and bring my father here with all speed."

With that he embraced his brother Benjamin around the neck and wept, and Benjamin wept on his neck. He kissed all his brothers and wept upon them; only then were his brothers able to talk to him. (Gen. 45:13-15)

After the family was gleefully reunited in Egypt, the Bible reports that Jacob, his spirit revived, lived for another seventeen years and died at the ripe old age of 147.

As I see it, there are two main strategic elements in the story after Benjamin is brought to Joseph. The first concerns whether Joseph should continue his deception and test his brothers once again. The rationality of this, I presume, depends in part on how he thinks his brothers will act: will they betray Benjamin, as they once did him, or will they remain loyal and try to save their youngest brother in order to console their despondent father?

If this were an impersonal test in which Joseph had no material stake, it would not be a game. But Joseph very definitely has a stake and cares deeply about the outcome, particularly as it affects Benjamin—who had no part in his earlier abandonment and is his only full brother—and his father. If Joseph seriously believed that his brothers might fail his test, he conceivably would have tried to do something else to ensure the safety of his father and Benjamin.

So the question for Joseph was: Would his brothers abandon Benjamin and accept his offer to go free? As the story developed, this choice fell on a concerned Judah, whose decision after Joseph's offer might be modeled by the first fork of the game tree shown in figure 4.5.

I suggest that, without foreknowledge that Joseph was his long-lost brother and would at any moment reveal himself (as indicated by the lower branch of the game tree), it was still better for Judah to offer to substitute himself for Benjamin and become Joseph's slave

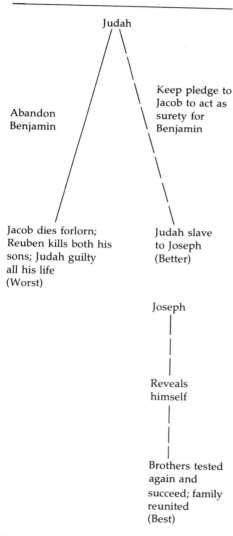

Key:
Ranking of outcomes is for Judah

Figure 4.5 Game tree of Joseph's offer to free brothers

than to walk away a free man. For his "freedom" would be purchased at a high price, given the promise he had made his father to act as surety for Benjamin; should he fail, his father could hold him guilty all his life, and his brother Reuben would have to kill his sons.

Thus, in figure 4.5, I have indicated Judah's acceptance of Joseph's offer of freedom to be "worst," his rejection as "better." Judah's (and Joseph's) "best" outcome occurs, of course, when Joseph reveals himself and the family is reunited. I have not indicated continuing deception as an option for Joseph in figure 4.5 because, as the Bible reports, Joseph was so moved by Judah's loyalty to Benjamin and their father that he probably never even considered testing his brothers anymore.

At the start of this second game, of course, Joseph did not know the lengths to which Judah and his other brothers had gone to assure their father that Benjamin would be safe in their company. Hence, it was still risky for him to use the device of a frame-up of Benjamin to test the brothers a second time. Why Joseph considered this an acceptable risk may be gleaned from his moralizing at the end:

God has sent me ahead of you to insure your survival on earth, and to save your lives in an extraordinary deliverance. So, it was not you who sent me here, but God; and He has made me a father [counselor] to Pharaoh, lord of all his household, and ruler over the whole land of Egypt. (Gen. 45:7-8)

A nice moral lesson on which to end this story, but it seems to me to hide the logic of the underlying strategic choices Joseph made.

4.5. Conclusions

I find Joseph's blanket assertion that a clairvoyant God made him prosperous and engineered his reconciliation with his brothers—or at least that the family would survive—unpersuasive. On the other hand, there is ample evidence that the conflict between Cain and Abel was God-inspired—God created a situation that was bound to lead to trouble. Jacob and Esau's struggle seems to lie somewhere between these earlier and later conflicts in the degree of God's involvement: He was able to predict something about the nature of their conflict at the prenatal stage but thereafter stayed out of touch, content apparently to let Rebekah manipulate events.

That the one story (Cain and Abel) in which God figures prominently—was clearly a player—does not have a happy ending for the family may say something about the consequences of His involvement. But before accusing God of always fouling up family affairs, recall the two sacrifice stories in chapter 3: from the role He played in each of these, it seems that His involvement may have been more or less salutary for His protagonists, depending on the strength of their faith (as I have defined it). Even when characters succeed without being blindly faithful, it may be presumed that they suffer from making agonizing calculations involving their children—and they will not quickly forget these nightmares.

Conflict within families is endemic in the Old Testament, and I have singled out for analysis in this chapter only three well-known stories from Genesis. Judging from the choices made by the biblical characters in these stories, their actions seem rational, if not always responsible, in these emotion-laden settings. In fact, it is the emotions that may overcome differences in the end—as was the case in the last two stories—pointing to the dual role of emotions as dividers and unifiers. Other family conflicts in which husband and wife, father and son, and uncle and niece lock horns will be analyzed in subsequent chapters.

It should be noted that conflict that cuts across generations is present in the Joseph story, wherein a dying father quarrels with his sons over the disposition of his favorite.

Indeed, this kind of conflict may transcend family considerations, as I shall show in a later story (section 7.3) when an older generation fights to hold onto the last vestiges of its power. First, however, I shall analyze an extended power struggle that began with God (and his human personification) confronting an intransigent Pharaoh, and then reconstituted itself as a conflict between God and the people with whom He originally allied Himself.

Protracted Conflict

5.1 Introduction

In one sense, all conflict in the Bible is protracted, for once one conflict ends another grows out of it, or new disruptive forces come into play. In fact, the Old Testament may be viewed as conflict piled upon conflict, with battles, wars, and family feuds the norm rather than the exception.

What makes a conflict "protracted," as I shall use this term, is that it not only spans time measured in generations but also involves one or more of the same characters over this extended time span. To be sure, old characters may leave and new characters enter, but there is a basic continuity provided by the trials and tribulations of at least one character.

The common character throughout the Bible is, of course, God, so I shall insist that a protracted conflict involve the continuing presence of someone else as well. That is, a conflict is *protracted* if it involves one (or more) human character(s) in games that span two or more generations. By this definition, Adam and Eve, though players in several games, did not play these games over a sufficiently long period to call their conflict protracted. Jacob, on the other hand, was involved with his brother, Esau, in early conflicts and (indirectly) with his son, Joseph, when he was an old man, so his family conflict was clearly extended in time. Yet, the character of this conflict changed so dramatically, and Jacob was such a remote player in the end, that I hesitate to label his family difficulties a single protracted conflict.

A protracted conflict that does have more internal coherence involved Moses from his birth to his death. Mostly taking the side of God, Moses first had an extended struggle with Pharaoh over the fate of the latter's Israelite slaves. After the demise of Pharaoh, Moses was preoccupied with keeping his people appeased, and on the side of God, for forty years while they wandered in the wilderness.

Moses's leadership problems were complicated in the beginning by his insecurity in his relationship with God, and by a growing independence and turning away from God in the end. Although Moses was never outrightly disloyal to God in his later years, he had constantly to suffer His wrath on account of his unruly charges, the Israelites. That Moses was largely successful in mollifying God attests both to his adroitness and God's perspicaciousness in designating him as leader.

In fact, as I shall show, God and Moses complemented each other

beautifully: as a foil for God's rashness, Moses was superb; as a user of Moses's conciliatory talents, God was exceptional. But more than being a good judge of character, God was able to visualize and then implement game scenarios—first with a defiant Pharaoh and then with the rebellious Israelites—that showed to great advantage His awesome power. God may not be omniscient, but on occasion He seems to show remarkable prescience.

This is quite a different picture from that sometimes painted of the God of Exodus, Numbers, and Deuteronomy, who often seems thoroughly frustrated by the turmoil that lasted from the captivity of the Israelites in Egypt to their entry into the promised land. But I believe the contrary is true: though suffering setbacks at one level, God enjoyed Himself enormously at another level in His expertly administered self-glorification campaign, which He could not have carried out without being continually challenged. Mean and dispirited as God seems as He copes with numerous antagonists in this protracted conflict, He in fact, I submit, looks for every good excuse to display His might. These are not lacking, as will be seen, and God, sovereign and seemingly invincible, exploits them with zeal.

5.2 Enter Moses

After Joseph and his brothers passed from the scene, a new generation of Israelites emerged that posed a serious threat to the existing order in Egypt:

The Israelites were fertile and prolific; they multiplied and increased very greatly so that the land was filled with them.

A new king arose over Egypt, who did not know Joseph. And he said to his people, "Look, the Israelite people are much too numerous for us. Let us deal shrewdly with them, so that they may not increase; otherwise in the event of war they may join our enemies in fighting against us and rise from the ground." (Exod. 1:7-10)

To deal with this threat of possible takeover, the Egyptians

set taskmasters over them to oppress them with forced labor; and they built garrison cities for Pharaoh: Pithom and Raamses. But the more they were oppressed, the more they increased and spread out, so that the [Egyptians] came to dread the Israelites. (Exod. 1: 11-12)

The Egyptians became even more cruel and ruthless, but to no avail. In desperation, Pharaoh decided that truly draconian measures were needed, so he ordered that Hebrew midwives kill newborn boys, presumably because females could better be assimilated into the Egyptian population, while males always posed the threat of overthrow.[1] Being God-fearing women, though, the midwives disobeyed Pharaoh's order, under the pretext that Hebrew women were more vigorous than Egyptian women and, while in labor, gave birth before the midwives could get to them.

Frustrated, Pharaoh then ordered that every newborn Hebrew boy be thrown into the Nile. But this sacrifice was unbearable for a certain Levite woman who bore a son:

When she saw how beautiful he was, she hid him for three months. When she could hide him no longer, she got a wicker basket for him and calked it with bitumen and pitch. She put the child into it and placed it among the reeds by the bank of the Nile. And his sister stationed herself at a distance, to learn what would befall him.

The daughter of Pharaoh came down to bathe in the Nile, while her maidens walked along the Nile. She spied the basket among the reeds and sent her slave girl to fetch it. When she opened it, she saw that it was a child, a boy crying. She took pity on it and said, "This must be a Hebrew child." (Exod. 2: 2-6)

Happily, when the boy's sister asked Pharaoh's daughter if she would like assistance, she said yes; the sister then sought out her mother, standing nearby, to care for her son. Pharaoh's daughter adopted the boy and called him Moses.

This touching story not only illustrates the ambivalence within Pharaoh's household but, as a literary device, works well to compound the irony in the next episode in Moses's life. Now fully grown, Moses observed an Egyptian strike a Hebrew:

He [Moses] turned this way and that and, seeing no one about, he struck down the Egyptian and hid him in the sand. When he went out the next day, he found two Hebrews fighting; so he said to the offender, "Why do you strike your fellow?" He retorted, "Who made you chief and ruler over us? Do you mean to kill me as you killed the Egyptian?" (Exod. 2:12–14)

"Frightened" (Exod. 2:14) by this response, Moses, who had thought that his murder of the Egyptian had gone undetected, quickly made a sagacious calculation: "Then the matter is known" (Exod. 2:14)!

The game player in Moses was correct: word had gotten to Pharaoh of the murder, and he tried to kill Moses. But Moses succeeded in escaping by fleeing to Midian, where he eventually married and raised a family. Yet he regretted he had become "a stranger in a foreign land" (Exod. 2:22).

Years passed, the old Pharaoh died, but

the Israelites were groaning under the bondage and cried out; and their cry for help from the bondage rose up to God. God heard their moaning, and God remembered His covenant with Abraham and Isaac and Jacob. God looked upon the Israelites, and God took notice of them. (Exod. 2:23–25)

God then singled out Moses for the task of delivering the Israelites from slavery, but Moses needed considerable convincing. Patiently, God offered various reassurances: He recreated Himself in a burning bush not consumed by fire; He told a reluctant Moses, "I will be with you" (Exod. 3:12) and "I have taken note of you and of what is being done to you in Egypt" (Exod. 3:16); and He provided Moses with detailed instructions on what to say to Pharaoh when he saw him.

But Moses still could not believe that he was up to the task. So for good measure God performed a few more miracles that He told Moses he himself could reenact to convince Pharaoh—as well as his own people—that he was indeed God's duly appointed representative. God even assuaged Moses's fear of not being "a man of words" (Exod. 4:10) by saying to him:

Who gives man speech? Who makes him dumb or deaf, seeing or blind? Is it not I, the LORD? Now go, and I will be with you as you speak and will instruct you what to say. (Exod. 4:11–12)

When Moses still protested his rhetorical inadequacies, God lost His patience and grew angry. Finally, He proposed a pragmatic solution:

There is your brother Aaron the Levite. He, I know, speaks readily. Even now he is setting out to meet you, and he will be happy to see you. You shall speak to him and put the words in his mouth—I will be with you and with him as you speak, and tell both of you what to do—and he shall speak for you to the people. Thus he shall serve as your spokesman, with you playing the role of God to him. And take with you this rod, with which you shall perform the signs. (Exod. 4:14–17)

The portrait of Moses that emerges is that of a meek man suffering almost debilitating doubts about his strength of character and physical capabilities. He is a constant worrier and continually seeks reassurance. I judge Moses at this point in his career to be a vacillating figure with an almost morbid aversion to becoming entrapped in a situation that entails substantial risk. Basically, he seems inept.

5.3 *God the Agent Provocateur*

In the end, God's sedulous exhortations to Moses, and His resounding demonstrations of miraculous powers, seem to succeed in allaying Moses's doubts and fears. But before sending Moses on his way, God still finds it necessary to give a final reminder to His anxious servant:

When you return to Egypt, see that you perform before Pharaoh all the marvels that I have put within your power. (Exod. 4:21)

This reminder is given, bear in mind, after a prior reminder to take the rod God had given him and had, in one of His previous miraculous demonstrations, turned into a snake and then back again.

If Moses is a pusillanimous figure who constantly needs reassurances and reminders, the same cannot be said for God. He seems to crave confrontation. Moreover, He is not above manipulating a situation so as to heighten the dramatic tension. After telling Moses to display all his marvels before Pharaoh, for example, He reveals a devious strategy for escalating the conflict with Pharaoh: "I, however, will stiffen his heart so that he will not let the people go" (Exod. 4:21).

This is blatant manipulation. Previously I showed (section 4.2) that

God had provoked Cain into murdering his brother by accepting Abel's offering while refusing Cain's, thereby implanting terrible jealousy in Cain. But that was manipulation of the physical circumstances of the situation. Now God seems ready to practice some mind manipulation as well, contrary to the notion that man has free will (section 2.2).

I have no explanation for this new-found ability of God, though His reasons for using it seem rather clear (to be discussed later). In fact, the mind manipulation of Pharaoh is one of the few instances I have discovered in the Old Testament in which a human character is robbed of his free will and, as such, his ability to make his own choices. (For another instance, see Josh. 11:20.)

To be sure, Pharaoh in the end does change his mind and seems to act on his own volition, so God's control appears not to be total. Also, Moses, spokesman for God that he is in the beginning, later asserts his independence, so he, too, emerges as more than just a mouthpiece of God. Nonetheless, it must be stressed that, as in the Cain and Abel story, the deck is heavily stacked by God at the outset—and only later do His antagonists emerge as full-fledged game players.

God signals that He is in charge, and beyond the control of any other forces, when He offers the following elliptic response to Moses's question of what to tell the Israelites if they ask God's name: "Ehyeh-Asher-Eyeh [I Am That I Am]" (Exod. 3:14). God amplifies this rather cryptic statement by saying:

Thus shall you say to the Israelites, "Ehyeh [I Am] sent me to you." And God said further to Moses, "Thus shall you speak to the Israelites: The LORD, the God of your fathers, the God of Abraham, the God of Isaac, and the God of Jacob, has sent me to you:

This shall be My name forever,
This My appellation for all eternity." (Exod. 3:14–15)

If the legitimate bases of God's authority are not exactly transparent from His "I Am That I Am" statement, then the next phase of the story offers some clues. While God may like to turn aside existential questions like Moses's with enigmatic responses, He is not so successful in covering up His role in human affairs when He is called upon to act.

This point is well illustrated after Moses and Aaron approach Pharaoh, and Moses entreats him with the words of "the LORD, the God of Israel" (Exod. 5:1):

Let My people go so that they may celebrate a festival for Me in the wilderness. (Exod. 5:1)

Pharaoh's mocking reply is:

Who is the LORD that I should heed Him and let Israel go? I do not know the LORD, nor will I let Israel go. (Exod. 5:2)

Pharaoh then follows up his reply by ordering that the Israelites no longer be provided with straw for making bricks but that the daily quota of bricks to be produced remain the same. When the quotas are not met, the Israelite foremen are beaten, and in a rage Pharaoh accuses them of shirking.

Upon leaving Pharaoh, the maligned foremen meet Moses and Aaron, who are waiting for them. They curse their ostensible benefactors and charge them with betrayal:

May the LORD look upon you and punish you for making us loathsome to Pharaoh and his courtiers—putting a sword in their hands to slay us. (Exod. 5:21)

Moses and Aaron indeed would seem to have good reason to question the perverse effects of their actions.

With the situation looking bleak, Moses implores God:

O Lord, why did You bring harm upon this people? Why did You send me? Ever since I came to Pharaoh to speak in Your name, he has dealt worse with this people; and still You have not delivered Your people. (Exod. 5:22-23)

God's answer now reveals more of His grand design:

You shall soon see what I will do to Pharaoh: he shall let them go because of a greater might; indeed, because of a greater might he shall drive them from his land. (Exod. 6:1)

Thus, a harsh Pharaoh and counterproductive appeals to him by Moses and Aaron are but preliminaries to the main event.

Before the main event begins, the Bible offers a key insight into God's rationale for staging the preliminaries that I have described. After repeating his earlier pledge to renew His covenant with Abraham, Isaac, and Jacob, and then reaffirming His pledge to rescue the Israelites from slavery, God speaks of His own role in the rescue operation:

I am the LORD. I will free you from the burdens of the Egyptians and deliver you from their bondage. I will redeem you with an outstretched arm and through extraordinary chastisements. And I will take you to be My people, and I will be your God. And you shall know that I, the LORD, am your God who freed you from the labors of the Egyptians. (Exod. 6:6–7)

Note the connection between the subjects of these two verses—six first-person references, modified by God's self-identification twice as "the LORD" and twice as "God"— with the verbs "free," "deliver," and "redeem." Not only can there be no doubt about who is doing all these things, but God also does not hide His opinion that His chastisements will be "extraordinary," that His efforts "you shall know." If His place in the universe were not already apparent, God concludes the next verse with a final "I the LORD" (Exod. 6:8).

Why does God so relentlessly hammer away at His self-designated role as savior of the Israelites? I believe there are at least two reasons. First, He probably anticipates—not without reason—future trouble with the people He has chosen to adopt, and the previously quoted statements help to establish His magnanimity when they were in desperate straits. Second, and more immediate, God, as I indicated earlier, continually seeks praise and admiration, and what better way is there to achieve it than to "free . . . deliver . . . redeem" a desperate people? Clearly, the sal-

vation of the Israelites becomes the more praiseworthy and admirable the more horrendous their condition is. Unwittingly, Moses and Aaron succeeded in aggravating it. In my opinion, it is all in God's design first to exacerbate an already deplorable situation for His chosen people and then to come gallantly to their rescue.

In game-theoretic terms, God is in a game of total conflict (see section 2.4) with Pharaoh—which I shall not try formally to elaborate at this point—so what is worst for Pharaoh is best for Him. The Israelites, and Moses and Aaron, may be temporarily hurt by a Pharaoh who brutalizes the slaves he fears, but the game God wants ultimately to win involves an objective other than just release of the slaves—God wants to magnify His achievements to the nth degree.

There is one troublesome question in this interpretation. Except for reasons of deep insecurity, it is not apparent why God does not let His great deeds speak for themselves instead of running on ad nauseam about His accomplishments. The only explanation I can think of is one alluded to earlier: anticipating that the Israelites will later deviate, He wants to get His "extraordinary chastisements" (Exod. 6:6) on the record.

Whatever the reasons for God's

unabashed insistence on His power and glory, it is evident that He sets the stage for a climactic confrontation that He thinks will enhance His image. I shall show next how, specifically, God orchestrates events to achieve this objective.

5.4 The Main Event

I have argued that God conveys by His words more than a simple respect for abiding by the terms of a covenant. He makes unmistakably clear that He alone is the LORD, and that He also determines the rules of the game.

That God is the only consequential player in this game is made manifest in an alternative account of the instructions God gives Moses before he and Aaron meet Pharaoh:

See, I place you in the role of God to Pharaoh, with your brother Aaron as your prophet. You shall repeat all that I command you, and your brother Aaron shall speak to Pharaoh to let the Israelites depart from his land. But I will harden Pharaoh's heart, that I may multiply My signs and marvels in the land of Egypt. When Pharaoh does not heed you, I will lay My hand upon Egypt and deliver My ranks, My people the Israelites, from the land of Egypt with extraordinary chastisements." (Exod. 7:1–4)

Note the repetition of the self-laudatory phrase "with extraordinary chastisements."

When Pharaoh proves "stubborn" (Exod. 7:14)—despite a demonstration by Aaron of his ability to turn his staff into a serpent that then swallows up serpents conjured up by Pharaoh's magicians—God escalates the conflict. Progressively, through Moses and Aaron, He brings harsher and harsher plagues down upon the Egyptians. Although the Egyptian magicians, through their spells, succeed in duplicating the first two plagues—turning the Nile into blood and infesting the land with frogs—after the second plague Pharaoh acknowledges God's existence and gains relief from the frogs only by promising to let the Israelites go to give sacrifice to their God.

Pharaoh retracts, however, and becomes once again obdurate. Successive plagues of lice, swarms of insects, pestilence against animals, dust that produces boils, thunder and hail, locusts, and darkness, which Pharaoh's magicians are no longer able to reproduce, each time induce Pharaoh to yield—but only temporarily. Then Pharaoh becomes implacable again—as God predicted he would—and thereby brings on himself and the Egyptians a new and more ghastly plague.

The hail of the seventh plague,

which levels everything in the open, destroying "man and beast and all the grasses of the field" (Exod. 9:22), strikes fear of God even in some of Pharaoh's courtiers. This is the first sign that their sufferance is not inexhaustible. The darkness of the ninth plague "that can be touched" (Exod. 10:21)—implying that even breathing becomes difficult in the palpable gloom—so enrages Pharaoh that he threatens Moses with death:

Be gone from me! Take care not to see me again, for the moment you look upon my face you shall die. (Exod. 10:28)

Moses responds by signaling that the climax is near:

You have spoken rightly. I shall not see your face again! (Exod. 10:29)

The coup de grace comes with the tenth plague, which God tells Moses will be the last:

Toward midnight I will go forth among the Egyptians, and every first-born in the land of Egypt shall die, from the first-born of Pharaoh who sits on his throne to the first-born of the slave girl who is behind the mill-stones; and all the first-born of the cattle. And there shall be a loud cry in all the land of Egypt, such as has

never been or will ever be again; but not a dog shall snarl at any of the Israelites, at man or beast—in order that you may know that the LORD makes a distinction between Egypt and Israel. (Exod. 11:4–7)

True to His word, "there was a loud cry in Egypt; for there was no house where there was not someone dead" (Exod. 12:30). Pharaoh could withstand the devastating effects of the plagues no longer and summoned Moses and Aaron:

Up, depart from among my people, you and the Israelites with you! Go, worship the LORD as you said! Take also your flocks and your herds, as you said, and begone! And may you bring blessing upon me also! (Exod. 12:31–32)

A fitting testimony to the sway God finally holds over even His enemies.

But what, exactly, is the game God is playing with Pharaoh? I previously showed Him to play a kind of assurance game with Moses to bolster the latter's courage and resolve for the main event. Then, after Moses and Aaron aggravated the situation for the Israelites, God offered reassurances. In the climactic struggle with Pharaoh that ensued, the question that needs to be answered, I believe, is why God unleashed the series of plagues that He did. After all, if He had full control over Pharaoh's mind, would it not have been easier and more expeditious for Him to have made Pharaoh yield quickly rather than endure the horror of ten hideous plagues?

The reason God desired a protracted conflict is hinted at in His several boastful statements quoted earlier about acting as savior of the Israelites in their time of crisis (which God, of course, had helped to deepen and prolong). But God also had another purpose in mind, which He expressed to Moses and Aaron just prior to their audience with Pharaoh (the first part of God's instructions were quoted at the beginning of this section):

And the Egyptians shall know that I am the LORD, when I stretch out My hand over Egypt and bring out the Israelites from their midst. (Exod. 7:5)

In other words, God did not just want to save His chosen people, which He could have done well enough by making Pharaoh less stubborn and more compassionate. He also wanted to teach Pharaoh and the Egyptians a lesson, which He seems to have succeeded in doing after the tenth plague. Indeed, not only did Pharaoh ask for God's blessing, as I indicated ear-

lier, but the Egyptians themselves hastened the exodus:

The Egyptians urged the people [Israelites] on, to make them leave in haste, for they said, "We shall all be dead." . . . And the LORD had disposed the Egyptians favorably toward the people, and they let them have their request; thus they stripped the Egyptians. (Exod. 12:33–36)

So were the tables turned on the Egyptians.

The (one-person) game God played with Pharaoh can be modeled as shown in figure 5.1. God's two strategy choices are to stop or to continue the plagues. Pharaoh, by contrast, does not really have strategy choices, as in a genuine two-person game. Rather, since God controls his behavior, he can better be thought of as a "state of nature"; his two possible states are to be "submissive" or "defiant (up to a point)."

These states do not arise strictly by chance, however, as is commonly assumed in decision theory; they are themselves chosen by God. Thus, God in effect can choose both a strategy—to stop or to continue the plagues—and a state of nature—to make Pharaoh submissive or defiant (up to a point).

The consequences of each pair of His choices (of one strategy and one

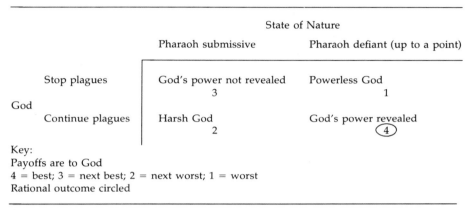

		State of Nature	
		Pharaoh submissive	Pharaoh defiant (up to a point)
	Stop plagues	God's power not revealed 3	Powerless God 1
God			
	Continue plagues	Harsh God 2	God's power revealed ④

Key:
Payoffs are to God
4 = best; 3 = next best; 2 = next worst; 1 = worst
Rational outcome circled

Figure 5.1 Payoff matrix to God in one-person game with Pharaoh

state of nature) are briefly described in figure 5.1. If God stops the plagues, He obtains His next-best outcome (3) when Pharaoh also cooperates by being submissive, His worst outcome (1) when Pharaoh remains defiant. The latter outcome obtains because God is shown to be powerless in the face of Pharaoh's defiance.

By continuing the plagues, on the other hand, God would appear harsh, his next-worst outcome (2), if Pharaoh were submissive, but he would obtain his best outcome (4) if Pharaoh remained defiant (up to a point). I say this latter outcome is best for God because His power would be fully revealed by His prolonged punishment of a defiant Pharaoh; if Pharaoh in the end capitulated—as actually happened—

then an unforgettable lesson would be transmitted to future generations about the futile consequences of defying God.

God taught this painful lesson to Pharaoh by making the appropriate row and column choices in figure 5.1 (second row, second column). From the passages I quoted earlier, moreover, it seems to have been taken to heart by both Pharaoh and his Egyptian subjects. But the game with Pharaoh is not quite over, as I shall show next, because Pharaoh soon has a change of heart and emerges as a new player, seemingly now out of God's mental reach.

5.5 A New Challenge

In section 5.4 I looked at the God-Pharaoh confrontation solely from

God's viewpoint, on the assumption that God held all the cards. But the story can also be read as one in which Pharaoh eventually reached the point where dogged defiance appeared futile, or at least no better than suicide in installments. Under this interpretation, Pharaoh, though rendered obstinate by God, in the end asserted his independence from God's control and made the rational calculation that it was in his own best interest to let the Israelites go.

This is why in figure 5.1 I have attributed to God the power to make Pharaoh "defiant," but only "up to a point." God's mastery of the situation loses its force when Pharaoh caves in, which is an interpretation more consistent with Pharaoh's possessing free will and making his own prudent choice.

But does Pharaoh act prudently, or is it part of God's larger design to have Pharaoh suffer a temporary setback only to reemerge as a more defiant protagonist whom God can then stamp out once and for all, without fear of being condemned as merciless? The Bible seems contradictory on this point. On the one hand, as the Israelites flee Egypt, God manipulates the situation so that

Pharaoh will say of the Israelites, "They are astray in the land; the wilderness has closed in on them." Then

I will stiffen Pharaoh's heart and he will pursue them, that I may assert My authority against Pharaoh and all his host; and the Egyptians shall know that I am the LORD. (Exod. 14:3-4)

On the other hand, in the next verse, the Bible says that Pharaoh had good reasons, apart from observing the Israelites in difficult country, to pursue them:

When the king of Egypt was told that the people had fled, Pharaoh and his courtiers had a change of heart about the people and said, "What is this we have done, releasing Israel from our service?" (Exod. 14:5)

Not knowing whether or not Pharaoh is a tool of God, I propose to look at the pursuit game in two ways. First, consider the game as if Pharaoh were an independent player who must decide whether to pursue or not pursue the Israelites. God/Moses then must decide whether to help or not help the Israelites. The outcome matrix for this game is shown in figure 5.2, whose rankings I justify as follows:

New confrontation (2,4): the next-worst outcome for Pharaoh, for even though the loss of the Israelite slaves would be catastrophic to Egypt, he risks a great deal in a new confrontation with God/Moses; the best outcome for God/Moses, for

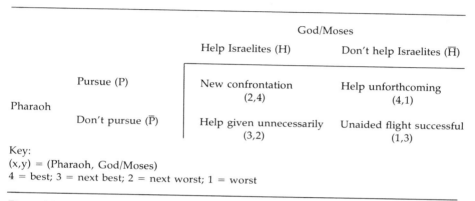

		God/Moses	
		Help Israelites (H)	Don't help Israelites (H̄)
Pharaoh	Pursue (P)	New confrontation (2,4)	Help unforthcoming (4,1)
	Don't pursue (P̄)	Help given unnecessarily (3,2)	Unaided flight successful (1,3)

Key:
(x,y) = (Pharaoh, God/Moses)
4 = best; 3 = next best; 2 = next worst; 1 = worst

Figure 5.2 Outcome matrix in pursuit game

they (especially God) relish the opportunity to display their power.

Help unforthcoming (4,1): the best outcome for Pharaoh, for he sees his victory as an easy one against the unarmed Israelites; the worst outcome for God/Moses, for they do not come to the aid of the Israelites in distress.

Help given unnecessarily (3,2): the next-best outcome for Pharaoh, because he would prefer not to pursue the Israelites when they are protected by God/Moses; the next-worst outcome for God/Moses, because they would be aiding a people quite capable of fending for themselves (when not pursued).

Unaided flight successful (1,3): the worst outcome for Pharaoh, because he could have regained the Israelite slaves without serious opposition; the next-best outcome for God/Moses, because the Israelites escape, though without benefit of another display of God/Moses's power.

Because Pharaoh makes his choice of whether to pursue the Israelites before God/Moses decide whether to come to their aid, the proper representation of the pursuit game is as a 2 × 4 payoff matrix (figure 5.3). In this game, God/Moses's tit-for-tat strategy is dominant; anticipating this choice, Pharaoh would pursue the Israelites, even though he obtains only his next-worst outcome.

The "rationality" of this outcome for Pharaoh would seem doubtful in view of what actually happened in the pursuit game. As the Egyptians bore down on the Israelites, Moses responded to their cries:

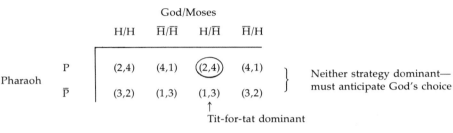

Figure 5.3 Payoff matrix in pursuit game

Have no fear! Stand by, and witness the deliverance which the LORD will work for you today; for the Egyptians whom you see today you will never see again. The LORD will battle for you; you hold your peace! (Exod. 14:13–14)

Indeed, with the help of God, Moses parted the Red Sea before the Israelites and, as soon as they had safely crossed it, directed that the water flow back. The entire Egyptian army was swallowed up in its waters.

In retrospect, Pharaoh's tenacious pursuit of the Israelites was for him an unmitigated disaster, but I would argue that he could not possibly have anticipated this outcome when he made his strategy choice. At worst, I believe, Pharaoh might have anticipated something

on the order of the plagues, each of which at least provided a warning of worse things to come. It would have been riskier, I assume, for Pharaoh to have suffered the loss of the slaves without a fight, which might have led the Egyptians to rise up in anger against him and perhaps depose or kill him.

By contrast, prospects of recapturing the Israelites did not look inauspicious. In fact, as the Egyptians closed in on the petrified Israelites, the Israelites were on the verge of deserting their leader:

Greatly frightened, the Israelites cried out to the LORD. And they said to Moses, "Was it for want of graves in Egypt that you brought us to die in the wilderness? What have you done to us, taking us out of Egypt? Is this not the very thing we told you in Egypt, saying, 'Let us be, and we will serve the Egyptians, for it is better for us to serve the Egyptians than to die in the wilderness'?'' (Exod. 14:10-12)

Furthermore, even after God threw the Egyptians into a panic by locking their chariot wheels as they crossed the parted sea, they were not beyond making a clearheaded calculation that they thought might save them:

Let us flee from the Israelites, for the LORD is fighting for them against Egypt. (Exod. 14:25)

But by then it was too late.

Now counterpose this interpretation of a rational Pharaoh and calculating Egyptians against God's preview of the whole affair:

And I will stiffen the hearts of the Egyptians so that they go in after them; and I will assert My authority against Pharaoh and all his warriors, his chariots and his horsemen. Let the Egyptians know that I am the LORD, when I assert My authority against Pharaoh, his chariots, and his horsemen. (Exod. 14:17-18)

Without contesting God's own glory-seeking motives, which I believe to be completely consistent with His previous behavior, it now must be asked whether a one-person interpretation of the pursuit game, with God as the sole player, is consistent with the outcome. Specifically, if God had made Pharaoh's strategy choice for him, would He have made the same choice Pharaoh did in the pursuit game?

This question can be answered by deleting Pharaoh's preferences from the outcome matrix in figure 5.2. Then, assuming Pharaoh's "choices" are really states of nature that God controls, as in figure 5.1, what would God do? Obviously, based on His preferences, God would have Pharaoh pursue the Israelites—in His terms, make Pharaoh and the Egyptians "obstinate"—and then help the Israelites, as actually occurred, resulting in a new confrontation that leads to His best outcome. In this manner, a manipulative God, effectively controlling Pharaoh's thoughts and actions, can also be used to explain what happened in the pursuit game.

Thus, the game-theoretic analysis does not distinguish whether Pharaoh was truly his own man, as suggested by the two-person interpretation, or was just a puppet of God, as suggested by the one-person interpretation. Both interpretations "work" in the sense of explaining the outcome that occurred in the pursuit game.

My own predisposition is toward the two-person interpretation, which endows Pharaoh with free will, since it is consistent with the place reserved for man in the world God initially created (see section 2.2). Nevertheless, I see a case can be made for the puppet interpretation, particularly in the earlier game played over the continuation of the plagues. Perhaps the truth lies somewhere in between: while Pharaoh was never really his own man, he exhibited greater independence in his later confrontation with God/Moses. His increasing self-assertiveness, I would add, seems also undergirded by a shrewd rationality.

5.6 Dissension in the Ranks

Pharaoh was not the only one to have become more assertive. Increasingly, Moses, in his dealings with Pharaoh, shed the apprehensions and fears he had suffered earlier in his career. But it is only after the demise of Pharaoh and the Egyptian army, when Moses faced unexpected internal challenges, that he emerged as a strong and independent figure.

As usual, God set the stage for later trouble by laying down "a fixed rule" (Exod. 15:25) designed to test the Israelites, now wandering in the wilderness:

If you will heed the LORD your God diligently, doing what is upright in His sight, giving ear to His commandments and keeping all His laws, then I will not bring upon you any of the diseases that I brought upon the Egyptians, for I the LORD am your healer. (Exod. 15:26)

Moses does not have long to wait before the Israelites start grumbling about conditions in the wilderness. First, there is not enough bread to eat, which God rectifies by raining down bread from the heaven. Then, when there is no water, God through Moses provides for it. God also helps Joshua, a close associate of Moses, defeat the attacking Amalekites.

Although the Israelites are not immune to disobedience, as when some of them fail to observe the sabbath, there is no serious challenge to God until three months after their departure from Egypt, when they arrive at Mount Sinai:

Now Mount Sinai was all in smoke, for the LORD had come down upon it in fire; the smoke rose like the smoke of a kiln, and the whole mountain trembled violently. The blare of the horn grew louder and louder. As Moses spoke, God answered him in thunder. The LORD came down upon Mount Sinai, on the top of the mountain, and the LORD called Moses to the top of the mountain and Moses went up. (Exod. 19:18–20)

Moses, and later Aaron, are the only people allowed to ascend the mountain. In the miasma enveloping Mount Sinai, God then speaks; His words are the Ten Commandments, the basic laws to which He demands adherence if the covenant is to be consummated and Israel is to become a "holy nation" (Exod. 19:6).

God next relates to Moses in considerable detail the rules that must be followed and the punishments for disobedience. Also, Moses is given meticulous instructions on the building of the Tabernacle, the sacred sanctuary for the worship of God.

Only after Moses ascends the mountain once again, this time to stay for forty days and nights, do the people become restless:

When the people saw that Moses was so long in coming down from the mountain, the people gathered against Aaron and said to him, "Come, make us a god who shall go before us, for that man Moses, who brought us from the land of Egypt—we do not know what happened to him." (Exod. 32:1)

Then Aaron became involved in a serious breach of faith, only later to try to retract. He told the people:

"Take off the gold rings that are on the ears of your wives, your sons, and your daughters, and bring them to me." And all the people took off the gold rings that were in their ears and brought them to Aaron. This he took from them and cast in a mold, and made it into a molten calf. And they exclaimed, "This is your god, O Israel, who brought you out of the land of Egypt!" When Aaron saw this, he built an altar before it; and Aaron announced: "Tomorrow shall be a festival of the Lord!" (Exod. 32:2–5)

The revelry of the people at the base of the mountain infuriated God, who commanded Moses:

Hurry down, for your people, whom you brought out of the land of Egypt, have acted basely. They have been quick to turn aside from the way that I enjoined upon them. They have made themselves a molten calf and bowed low to it and sacrificed to it, saying, "This is your god, O Israel, who brought you out of the land of Egypt!" (Exod. 32:7–8)

The next exchange between God and Moses firmly establishes Moses as his own man:

The LORD further said to Moses, "I see that this is a stiffnecked people. Now, let Me be, that My anger may blaze forth against them and that I may destroy them, and make of you a great nation." But Moses implored the LORD his God, saying, "Let not

Your anger, O Lord, blaze forth against Your people, whom You delivered from the land of Egypt with great power and a mighty hand. Let not the Egyptians say, 'It was with evil intent that He delivered them, only to kill them off in the mountains and annihilate them from the face of the earth.'" (Exod. 32:9-12)

As rhetorical questions a defense attorney might ask, the entreaties of Moses highlight the issue that God, acting as judge, must decide. Given the commitment to Israel He has made, and given also that this commitment is now well known, is it rational for God at this juncture to brush aside His handiwork out of pique?

This is the nub of the matter for God, as Moses brilliantly perceives. On this Moses now builds a cogent defense:

Turn from Your blazing anger, and renounce the plan to punish Your people. Remember Your servants, Abraham, Isaac, and Jacob, how You swore to them by Your Self and said to them: I will make your offspring as numerous as the stars of heaven, and I will give to your offspring this whole land of which I spoke, to possess forever. (Exod. 32:12-13)

God, who had earlier recalled in a heavenly metaphor to Moses "how

I bore you [children of Israel] on eagles' wings and brought you to Me" (Exod. 19:4), could not turn down this plea, and He relented.

God thus comes off as quick-tempered but not unmerciful. He is, in His own words, an "impassioned god" (Exod. 20:5), but He is also compassionate, perhaps even sentimental. It must be stressed, however, that given God's enormous investment in His chosen but "stiff-necked" people, and His strong desire not to destroy His credibility by reneging on His commitment to them, this "merciful" decision is by no means a fatuous one.

But now Moses is caught in a bind. After his intercession before God, he approached the camp of the Israelites, carrying two tablets on which the Ten Commandments were inscribed. When he "saw the calf and the dancing" (Exod. 32:19), he was enraged:

He hurled the tablets from his hands and shattered them at the foot of the mountain. He took the calf that they had made and burned it; he ground it to powder and strewed it upon the water and so made the Israelites drink it. (Exod. 32:19-20)

Moses next wrung a confession out of Aaron for his part in the idolatrous affair. Then, seeing that the people were "out of control" (Exod.

32:25), Moses tried to avert catastrophe by seizing the initiative: "Whoever is for the LORD, come here" (Exod. 32:26)!

Moses's gamble paid off, at least for one tribe in the donnybrook:

And all the Levites rallied to him. He said to them, "Thus says the LORD, the God of Israel: Each of you put sword on thigh, go back and forth from gate to gate throughout the camp, and slay brother, neighbor, and kin." The Levites did as Moses had bidden; and some three thousand of the people fell that day. And Moses said, "Dedicate yourselves to the LORD this day—for each of you has been against son and brother—that He may bestow a blessing upon you today." (Exod. 32:26–29)

When Moses then asked that God pardon the people for their sins, God was forgiving, but not without promising later retribution.

As I see the conflict at Mount Sinai, it involved God, Moses, and the Israelites in a three-player game, whose moves are depicted in the game tree of figure 5.4. The game begins with Moses's entreaty to God to be merciful; if He is, Moses then must decide whether to act forcefully, destroying the tablets and demanding sacrifice, or minimize the deviations of the Israelites. Given that Moses acts forcefully,

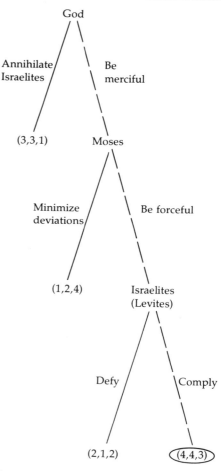

Key:
(x,y,z) = (God, Moses, Israelites)
4 = best; 3 = next best; 2 = next worst;
1 = worst
Circled outcome rational

Figure 5.4 Game tree of dissension at Mount Sinai

the Israelites—with the Levites distinguished from the rest—must decide whether to comply with Moses's demands or defy them.

At the four endpoints of the game tree in figure 5.4, I have ranked the outcomes associated with the choices of each player from best to worst. For purposes of decision, the relevant ranks are those associated with the player making the decision at each fork.

Starting with the Israelites (Levites) at the bottom of the tree, I assume that they prefer compliance (3), even if it entails sacrifice, over defiance (2), which could lead to their complete annihilation in line with God's earlier threat to Moses. They would, of course, most prefer that Moses minimize their deviations, given no further reprisals are taken against them (4), and least prefer that God annihilate the nation entirely (1).

Given that the Israelites comply with God's demand for sacrifice, Moses would prefer to act forcefully and destroy the tablets (4) than minimize their deviations (2), especially after having pleaded their case before God. The worst outcome for Moses would be to have the Israelites then defy him (1), whereas his next-best outcome would be to have God carry out His initial threat (3); in the case of the latter, Moses could at least rest assured that he had done his best to

save his people, while looking forward to being founder of a new "great nation" (Exod. 32:10) after their extermination.

Finally, God, given that He perceives that Moses will subsequently act forcefully—and the Israelites (Levites) will comply with his demands for sacrifice—would prefer to be merciful (4) rather than annihilate His chosen people (3). Worse for God would be to witness further defiance (2) or see his faithful servant, Moses, try to minimize the deviations of the Israelites (1).

For the preferences of the players I have assumed, the three-person game at Mount Sinai was played rationally by all parties. I would single out Moses's play as particularly masterful, first through his exceedingly clever defense of his people before God, then by his successful rallying of the Levites to his side after an electrifying display of anger.

5.7 More Dissension, More Retribution

Striking figure that Moses now cuts, he cannot, even with God's support, impose a stable order on, or evoke continuing contrition from, his people. His task, perhaps, is not always helped by a spiteful God, who instructs him to tell the Israelites:

You are a stiffnecked people. If I were to go in your midst for one moment, I would destroy you. Now, then, leave off your finery, and I will consider what to do to you. (Exod. 33:5)

God later followed up this implicit threat with a more magnanimous statement:

I will make all My goodness pass before you, and I will proclaim before you the name LORD, and the grace that I grant and the compassion that I show. (Exod. 33:19)

However, He showed how deep His animosity still ran when He said that He was one who

visits the iniquity of fathers upon children and children's children, upon the third and fourth generations. (Exod. 34:7)

Thus God, while someone of "grace" and "compassion," seems more ready to rely on imprecations and threats than promises.

Despite God's wariness and cynicism, He renewed the covenant with the Israelites and Moses delivered the Ten Commandments intact. The Israelites were asked to make sacrifices and bring offerings to God, and eventually the Tabernacle was completed.

The wanderings of the Israelites in the wilderness are next picked up in Numbers, where, characteristically, the Bible reports:

The people took to complaining bitterly before the LORD. The LORD heard and was incensed: a fire of the LORD broke out against them, ravaging the outskirts of the camp. The people cried out to Moses. Moses prayed to the LORD, and the fire died down. (Num. 11:1–2)

Further problems crop up, God's rancor grows, and a troubled Moses asks:

Why have You dealt ill with Your servant, and why have I not enjoyed Your favor, that You have laid the burden of all this people upon me? Did I conceive all this people, did I bear them, that You should say to me, "Carry them in your bosom as a nurse carries an infant," to the land that You have promised on oath to their fathers? (Num. 11:11–12)

As Cain rejected fraternal responsibility (section 4.2), Moses now abjures, metaphorically, maternal responsibility. Moses, however, is no intemperate Cain ready to wreak violence on the community. Rather, his lugubrious solution is to withdraw:

I cannot carry all this people by myself, for it is too much for me. If You would deal thus with me, kill me rather, I beg You, and let me see no more of my wretchedness! (Num. 11:14–15)

Moses's threat of withdrawal convinces God that His pious servant needs help, and he orders Moses to assemble seventy elders to share with him the burden of governance. God also squelches further grumblings against Moses, including some from Aaron and Moses's sister, Miriam.

After the land of Canaan, flowing "with milk and honey" (Num. 13:27), is explored, the people clamor to occupy the land, but it is inhabited by men of great size living in large and fortified cities. Once again the people despair of Moses and Aaron's leadership:

"If only we had died in the land of Egypt," the whole community shouted at them, "or if only we might die in this wilderness! Why is the LORD taking us to that land to fall by the sword? Our wives and children will be carried off! It would be better for us to go back to Egypt!" And they said to one another, "Let us head back for Egypt." (Num. 14:2–4)

But it is God who is most disturbed that the people "spurn" (Num. 14:11) Him, and it is Moses once again who intercedes on their behalf, repeating his argument that

God's credibility would be impaired if He retracted His oath to His chosen people. This time, though, God, while accepting Moses's plea to spare the Israelites, is not ambiguous about the punishment He intends:

None of the men who have seen My Presence and the signs that I have performed in Egypt and in the wilderness, and who have tried Me these many times and have disobeyed Me, shall see the land that I promised on oath to their fathers. (Num. 14:22–23)

More specifically,

not one shall enter the land in which I swore to settle you—save Caleb son of Jephunneh and Joshua son of Nun. Your children who, you said, would be carried off—these will I allow to enter; they shall know the land that you have rejected. But your carcasses shall drop in this wilderness, while your children roam the wilderness for forty years, suffering for your faithlessness, until the last of your carcasses is down in the wilderness. You shall bear your punishment for forty years, corresponding to the number of days—forty days—that you scouted the land: a year for each day. (Num. 14:30–34)

Fitting retribution, it seems, to ensure that "you shall know what it means to thwart Me" (Num. 14:34).

This punishment does not end trouble for Moses or God. Elements of the Israelites continue to voice complaints—even challenge Moses's authority again—and are summarily dispatched by a brooding God. As for Moses and Aaron, because God considers them to have been disloyal, "for, in the wilderness of Zin, when the community was contentious, you disobeyed My command" (Num. 27:14), they, too, are prevented from entering the promised land. Of all the men twenty years old or over who originally had fled Egypt, only Caleb and Joshua, who "remained loyal to the LORD" (Num. 32:12), are allowed to cross the Jordan River and set foot in Canaan. Indeed, it is Joshua, with Moses's blessing, who leads the Israelites into the land that God had promised their forefathers would be theirs.

Perhaps the central puzzle in the wanderings of the Israelites in the wilderness is how they were able to survive at all. Almost from the start, God was continually out of sorts and, frustrated by their misdeeds, ready on more than one occasion to wipe them out altogether. Their gross misbehavior at Mount Sinai, with the complicity of Aaron, occurred only three months after their departure from Egypt and involved a direct challenge to the first two of the Ten Commandments:

You shall have no other gods beside Me.

You shall not make for yourself a sculptured image, or any likeness of what is in the heavens above, or on the earth below, or in the waters under the earth. (Exod. 20:3–4)

My explanation for God's tolerance of the repeated transgressions of the Israelites is that it had little to do with any great compassion He felt for them. While they were His chosen people, and while He had made an oath to their forefathers to protect them, God found the progeny stubborn and generally disagreeable, if not downright wicked.

How does one deal with such an unfortunate state of affairs? In God's case, I believe, He looked for His solution in the best of the lot— Moses—with the hope of setting him up as their protector.

As I showed, however, God had to work hard in the beginning to convince a reluctant Moses that he was up to the task. But in the end, with his mettle established in the struggle with Pharaoh, Moses was ready and able to serve as a buffer between God and His chosen, if ungrateful and unregenerate, people.

Thus, I interpret Moses's primary role to be a foil for God's anger and explosive temper. God, in my opinion, understood that His patience would be tried to the limit by the querulous Israelites, and He wanted to provide them with a worthy protector to counter any precipitous actions He might take or even contemplate. As I have shown, Moses—until the end—served admirably in this role, interceding before God on several occasions to deflect His slashing anger and jealousy. Usually he would make his appeal by playing on God's vanity, reminding Him of how much would be lost in future credibility if he reneged on his oath and exterminated the Israelites.

Yet God could not morosely sit by and do nothing when challenged by egregious breaches of faith. Accordingly, He did punish the apostates after defaming them, but always, with prodding from a now-charismatic Moses, was persuaded to stop short of wiping the slate clean.

Often God tried to root out just the bad elements, but because these were ubiquitous, the job was never quite done. Even Moses, for all his integrity, did not escape unblemished in God's eyes, but that is probably an occupational hazard of a public defender who takes the side of—or at least is associated with—the criminal element in the face of such an imposing authority as God's. Nevertheless, as reported in Deuteronomy, Moses survived his difficult role with unique stature:

Never again did there arise in Israel a prophet like Moses—whom the LORD singled out, face to face, for the various signs and portents that the LORD sent him to display in the land of Egypt, against Pharaoh and all his courtiers and his whole country, and for all the great might and awesome power that Moses displayed before all Israel. (Deut. 34:10-12)

I believe the puzzle of a jealous but almost infinitely patient God is solved once one understands that God set up Moses to deal with intractable situations that He knew He would not be able to handle Himself. In particular, recognizing His own quick temper, God deliberately selected a man capable of defusing it. Thereby Moses acted not only as a kind of savior of his people from an all-but-certain debacle in Egypt but, just as important, as a guide in the wilderness for forty years. Although Moses was denied the reward of entering Canaan, he was "singled out, face to face" (Deut. 34:10) before God—which some have taken to mean that Moses was the only mortal ever to see God.[2]

In summary, I see all the major players in the wilderness game as acting rationally: God, in encouraging Moses to intercede on behalf of the Israelites to bring out the best in Him without at the same time undermining His future credibility; Moses, in accepting this role, albeit reluctantly at times, and finally receiving his unique reward; and the Israelites, in rebelling when conditions were difficult, sometimes having them alleviated but, even when not, always being saved from total destruction. In section 5.8 I shall conclude by trying to show how the protracted conflict that began with Moses's birth and ended with his death comprises a series of games bound together by a common set of strategic calculations.

5.8 Conclusions

If there is one character in the Bible with unexcelled prescience, it is God. Clearly, biblical characters are nobody's fools; however, God's place in the scheme of things is special, because He, more than any other character, is capable of setting up games He wishes to play. As I previously suggested, He does not seem quite omniscient, but He certainly is unique in His ability to plan His moves over an extended series of games.

This ability is more evident in the protracted conflict studied in this chapter than perhaps in any games heretofore analyzed, including those that began with the creation. Moses lived to be 120 years old, and from birth he was blessed. This is not to say that God took direct control of his early life, but the fact that Moses emerged relatively unscathed from a series of taxing en-counters, including murder, indicates that fate—or God's guiding hand—was not against him.

The Bible offers no reasons why Moses was chosen to lead the exodus from Egypt, though it says that Moses was an unhappy exile in a foreign land. Whatever the reason for God's choice, He assiduously coached a timorous and seemingly untalented Moses.

Perhaps God calculated that too threatening a figure might encourage Pharaoh to give up his slaves without a fight. In any event, the plodding Moses, with God's coaching and Aaron's forensic skills, did succeed after some early bungling in sustaining a rather grim game against Pharaoh in which God's power was publicized to the hilt, with plague after plague being visited upon this hapless but intransigent Egyptian.

That God manufactured the plagues to have their desired effect seems clear; what is less clear is that He later forced Pharaoh to pursue Moses and the Israelites by making him obstinate. What seems closer to the truth, as I argued, is that Pharaoh calculated that he had a good chance of intercepting the slaves while in flight; even if God intervened again on the side of the Israelites, he probably did not anticipate his own destruction, at least in one fell swoop. It therefore seems to me that while God largely established the rules of the game, Pharaoh did not act irrationally within the rules as he perceived them.

God's desire for self-glorification does not terminate with Pharaoh's elimination; this is only the prelude. The crucial last phase of the protracted conflict that God and his acolyte, Moses, are parties to, however, has both a different cast of characters and a different tone.

Now poised and politically adept, Moses does his best to control an unruly and ungrateful people. In time, though, he becomes disillusioned with and bitter about his middleman role and wants out. But just as Moses arrested God's intemperate predilections by courageously pleading for the salvation of the Israelites, God now reciprocates by giving his beleaguered disciple help that lightens his burden.

The most striking fact of this final phase of the conflict is not the alliance between God and Moses. This has existed throughout their long relationship. It is the change in the nature of their relationship, in which Moses emerges as his own man. The transformation of a daunting Moses into a strong and forceful personality is, I believe, exactly what God intended.[3] It makes Moses not just an acolyte but an independent, and thus more efficacious, champion of his people—about whom God has gotten very

upset, even if they provide Him an excuse for flexing His muscles to underscore his hegemony.

If Moses succeeds in saving his people in the end, God once again is still able to give magnificent displays of His might and power to keep the people generally in line. These exhibitions, in my opinion, He both needs and wants—and that is the fundamental similarity this final phase of the conflict has with the preceding phase involving the confrontation with Pharaoh. The cast of characters changes, but not God's aims, and even the stern means he uses to effect these aims. Thus, there is perhaps more constancy in the protracted conflict than first meets the eye, at least insofar as God is concerned.

If there is a new twist in the second phase of the conflict, it comes in Moses's metamorphosis from bumbling servant to self-assured and adroit spokesman for His people, which is in God's interest but a change He cannot quite live with comfortably. Hence God, while recognizing Moses's rectitude and supreme achievements, denies him a final resting place in Canaan.

6

Just Agreements and Wise Arbitration

6.1 Introduction

In this chapter I shall explore through three stories some strategic aspects of just and wise decisions in the Bible. Interestingly enough, two of the stories involve prostitutes, who one might think would be least able to illuminate questions of justice and wisdom. Yet it is often just such characters who are most clearheaded about the benefits and costs of their choices as they try to cope with a world that is not always willing to honor their services.

Prostitution, though, is not the central issue in these stories. It is, rather, the rationality of subscribing to agreements with other parties or placing a decision in the hands of an arbitrator trying to coax out the truth. Indeed, it is the lack of honesty on the part of some characters in all three stories discussed that makes problematic the rendering of just and wise decisions.

Strategic calculations when truthfulness is suspect are not only hard to make but also pose certain ethical dilemmas. For example, when it is evident that one character is not telling the truth, is it ethical to try to use deception as a weapon to ferret it out? If a party has been deceived, does he or she have a right to abrogate an agreement made as a result of being deceived?

The stories analyzed in this chapter raise these kinds of questions and demonstrate the close linkage between ethics and strategy. Two of the stories occur after the death of Moses, whom Joshua replaced as leader of the Israelites. The third takes place during the reign of Solomon, who ruled as king of Israel several generations later. In all three stories, I believe the strategic analysis clarifies ethical questions raised by the actions of the protagonists. I shall touch upon the philosophical implications of these questions in the final section of this chapter.

6.2 Rahab and the Spies

After the death of Moses, Joshua prepared for the occupation of Canaan by sending out two spies to reconnoiter the country:

They came to the house of a harlot named Rahab and lodged there. The king of Jericho was told, "Some men have come here tonight, Israelites, to spy out the country." The king of Jericho thereupon sent orders to Rahab: "Produce the men who came to you and entered your house, for they have come to spy out the whole country." (Josh. 2:1–3)

Rahab admitted to seeing the two men but said they had already left. She claimed not to know where they had gone but urged that they be pursued.

The pursuit was fruitless, because Rahab had in fact hidden the men on her roof among stalks of flax. The reason she gave to the spies for deceiving her king was based on exactly the kind of information that, as I argued in chapter 5, God intended to convey by His punitive actions:

I know that the LORD has given the country to you, because dread of you has fallen upon us, and all the inhabitants of the land are quaking before you. For we have heard how the LORD dried up the waters of the Sea of Reeds [Red Sea] for you when you left Egypt, and what you did to Sihon and Og, the two Amorite kings across the Jordan, whom you doomed. When we heard about it, we lost heart, and no man had any more spirit left because of you; for the LORD your God is the only God in heaven above and on earth below. (Josh. 2:9–11)

As a prostitute (and business woman), Rahab was certainly knowledgeable about the exchange of favors. Not intending to let her hiding of the spies go unrewarded, she put the following proposition to them:

Now, since I have shown loyalty to you, swear to me by the LORD that you in turn will show loyalty to my family. Provide me with a reliable sign that you will spare the lives of my father and mother, my brothers and sisters, and all who belong to them, and save us from death. (Josh. 2:12–13)

Recognizing a good deal when they saw one, the spies willingly accepted the proposition, but with the proviso that Rahab continue to support them.

Our persons are pledged for yours, even to death! If you will not disclose this mission of ours, we will show you true loyalty when the LORD gives us the land. (Josh. 2:14)

Abetting the escape of the spies from her roof, Rahab offered them some advice:

Make for the hills, so that the pursuers may not come upon you. Stay there in hiding three days, until the pursuers return; then go your way. (Josh. 2:16)

The spies, in turn, after reminding Rahab that their deal was binding only if she did exactly what they said, told her:

When we invade the country, you tie this length of crimson cord to the window through which you let us down. Bring your father, your mother, your brothers, and all your family together in your house. (Josh. 2:18)

Rahab followed their instructions to the letter, as the spies followed Rahab's advice. After hiding for three days in the hills, the spies escaped detection and returned safely to Joshua, reporting to him what had happened.

With not inconsequential assistance from God, Jericho was captured after the sound of ram's horns and the shouts of the Israelite army brought its walls crashing down. Before the city was destroyed by fire, the two spies led Rahab and her family to safety, "for she had hidden the messengers that Joshua sent to spy out Jericho" (Josh. 6:25).

As given by the outcome matrix in figure 6.1, there seems nothing very complex about the game played between Rahab and the spies. Rahab could either hide or not hide the spies; they could either save or not save Rahab after Jericho was taken (assuming that it was). Since Rahab had to make the first choice, it would appear that the proper representation of this game is as a 2 × 4 payoff matrix, in which the spies have four strategies, conditional on Rahab's two choices.

The problem with this representation is that it ignores some crucial steps in the sequence of moves, including the deal struck between Rahab and the spies and the fact that Rahab could still betray the spies after agreeing not to, and similarly,

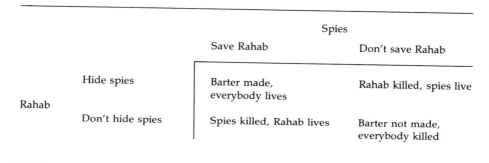

Figure 6.1 Outcome matrix of Rahab's game

they could betray her after she saved them. Also, if Rahab did not hide the spies, they would never have had the opportunity to make a choice of saving her or not, as assumed in figure 6.1 and in the 2 × 4 expansion of this outcome matrix. (In the 2 × 4 expansion, for example, the tat-for-tit strategy would say that after Rahab refuses to hide the spies, they would save her, which would be clearly impossible if they were dead!)

A more realistic representation of Rahab's game is as two nested subgames, shown in the revised representation in figure 6.2. In the first subgame, Rahab and the spies must decide whether to offer to barter their lives or not. (Since it is essentially a choice they make simultaneously, it can be represented as a 2 × 2 game.) If neither offers, I assume both players obtain their

next-worst outcome (2). If one offers and the other does not, I assume that the one who does not still obtains his next-worst outcome (2) because no barter is consummated; the one who offers, however—only to have his hopes dashed by the other player—receives his worst outcome (1).

If both players agree to the barter, the second subgame ensues, with payoff (x,y) as yet to be determined. Now Rahab has the first move: she may either keep the agreement or break it. If she keeps the agreement and the spies escape with their lives, they in turn can either save her or kill her by keeping or not keeping their side of the agreement.

If they keep their word, I assume both they and Rahab obtain their best outcome (4); if they betray Rahab, they live but are dishonored for allowing someone to be killed

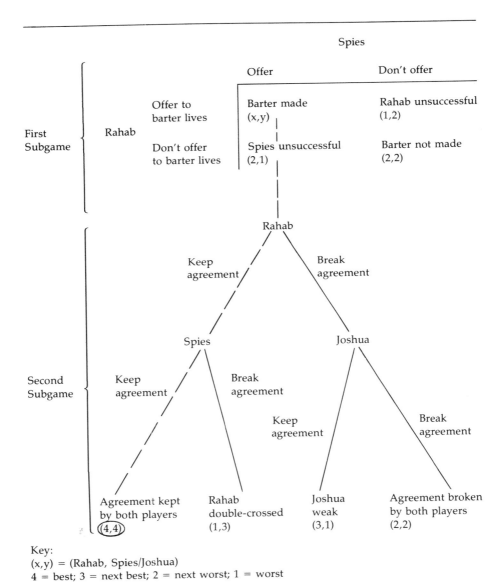

Key:
(x,y) = (Rahab, Spies/Joshua)
4 = best; 3 = next best; 2 = next worst; 1 = worst
Circled outcome rational

Figure 6.2 Rahab's game revised

who was loyal to them and had recognized their God as the only true God, which I take to be their next-best outcome (3). Rahab, who is double-crossed, receives her worst outcome (1).

Should Rahab not keep her agreement, the spies would be killed, and the choice would presumably fall on Joshua of whether or not to save Rahab (assuming he learned later of their betrayal). If he did not avenge the betrayal of his spies, I assume he would obtain his worst outcome (1), for he would be considered weak for not exacting retribution; Rahab would receive her next-best outcome (3) for living but suffering the guilt of her betrayal of the spies and possibly later retribution. (The later retribution might come if Joshua learned of her betrayal, because, like everybody else, Rahab and her family would presumably be killed when Jericho was destroyed.) Both players, I assume, would obtain their next-worst outcome (2) if they both broke the agreement, for it would be tantamount to not offering to barter in the first place.

Since the outcome chosen in the second subgame determines the rationality of bartering in the first subgame, prudence dictates that each player first determine the rational outcome in the second subgame. Plugging this outcome into the matrix of the first subgame

in figure 6.2, the players could then better ascertain a rational strategy choice in this subgame.

Starting with the bottom choices in the game tree of the second subgame in figure 6.2, the spies would prefer (4,4) to (1,3), and Joshua would prefer (2,2) to (3,1). Working up the tree, between (4,4) and (2,2) Rahab would prefer (4,4), so the rational choice of each player in the second subgame is to honor the agreement he (she) makes. The question now is: Should they make this agreement in the first place?

Given that the outcome of the second subgame will be (4,4), this outcome can be substituted for (x,y) in the matrix defining the first subgame in figure 6.2. However, while this substitution yields both players their best outcome (4) when they agree to barter their lives, it is not associated with a dominant strategy of either player, which neither has in this subgame after the substitution of (4,4) for (x,y). Thus, for example, while "offer" is better than "don't offer" for Rahab if the spies choose "offer," this is not true if the spies choose "don't offer," for "2" is better than "1" for Rahab in the spies' second column of figure 6.2.

Define a *superior outcome* to be one preferred by both players to any other outcome in a two-person game. In a game having such an outcome but in which neither player has a dominant strategy, I interpret this to be the rational outcome of tne game.

It is, however, rational in a weaker sense than an outcome associated with the dominant strategy of a player. To illustrate this point by the game in figure 6.2, if one player should act irrationally and either not return the other's offer or not keep his side of the agreement, the other player obtains his worst outcome (1). [If the other player had a dominant strategy in the first subgame, he could obtain at least his next-worst outcome (2).] Cognizant of this problem, I would nonetheless contend that in the composite game comprising the two subgames, it is rational for both players to barter their lives—and to do so in good faith, sticking to the agreement they make.

A notion of what constitutes a "just agreement" can be gleaned from Rahab's game. First, it must be voluntarily subscribed to, and second, it must be *stable*—invulnerable to violation by one or both players. By *invulnerable* I mean that neither player has an interest in violating an agreement once it is made, because he would suffer a worse outcome if he violated it, either by himself or together with the other player.

In Rahab's game, these conditions for a just agreement are clearly met: it was voluntarily subscribed to, and it was stable because, as the game-tree analysis demonstrated, either player would have done worse if he had violated the agreement. In fact, both players would have done worse, because the outcome (4,4), if lost in the second subgame because one or both players violated the agreement, also would have been lost in the prior first subgame, assuming both players had agreed in the first subgame to barter their lives.

It is easy to see that if the players in a composite game are rational, their assent to an agreement in the first subgame implies that the agreement is stable in subsequent subgames. For if it were not, at least one player would have an incentive to violate it; assuming a violation by one player hurts at least one other player, that other player would not give his assent to the agreement in the first place. Hence, it is sufficient to define a *just agreement* as one to which rational players would subscribe. If they did not, it would be because they anticipate a violation that would hurt them, thereby robbing them of any incentive even to begin negotiation.

Recall that, to secure Rahab's agreement, the spies had told Rahab their barter of lives was conditional on her adhering to their instructions. Indeed, after telling Rahab and her family to stay indoors during the capture of Jericho, the spies repeated their conditions, which Rahab accepted:

"If you disclose this mission of ours, we shall likewise be released from the oath which you made us take." She replied, "Let it be as you say." (Josh. 2:20-21)

Thus, the agreement in Rahab's game was rendered stable not just by a promise of the spies to keep it but by their avowal of revenge if they were betrayed. By inextricably linking their lives and Rahab's, the spies made it impossible for her to double-cross them with impunity, even though she could have struck the first blow by turning them in.

I shall next consider a case of an agreement that involved deception by one party to the agreement. Without deception, no agreement would have been made, so the agreement was by definition unjust. But in the end, the aggrieved party was able to implement the agreement in such a way that some of the sting was taken out of its deception.

6.3 Joshua's Deception by the Gibeonites

After the destruction of Jericho, Joshua next destroyed Ai, which struck fear in the inhabitants of Gibeon, a nearby people almost certain to face annihilation by the invading Israelites. To try to secure a peace treaty with the Israelites, the savvy Gibeonites adopted the ploy of pretending to be inhabitants of a distant country who had traveled a long way. The Israelites were suspicious of their disheveled appearance, though, especially since they were permitted to make peace only with those who lived at a great distance from them:

But perhaps you live among us; how then can we make a pact with you? (Josh. 9:7)

First countering with a concession—a willingness to be subjugated—the Gibeonites repeated their lie:

They said to Joshua, "We will be your subjects." But Joshua asked them, "Who are you and where do you come from?" They replied, "Your servants have come from a very distant country, because of the fame of the LORD your God." (Josh. 9:8-9)

The Gibeonites then added, revealingly, that it was not fame alone that impelled them but that they had heard "of all that He [God] did in Egypt" (Josh. 9:9).

The Gibeonites claimed to have proof of the great distance they traveled:

This bread of ours, which we took from our houses as provision, was still hot when we set out to come to you; and see how dry and crumbly it has become. These wineskins were new when we filled them, and see how they have cracked. These clothes and sandals of ours are worn out from the very long journey. (Josh. 9:12-13)

In the end, Joshua was taken in:

Joshua established friendship with them; he made a pact with them to spare their lives, and the [Israelite] chieftains of the community gave them their oath. (Josh. 9:15)

But three days after the treaty was granted, the Israelites learned the truth. Though outraged, they

did not attack them, since the chieftains of the community had sworn to them by the LORD, the God of Israel. (Josh. 9:18)

It was a moral precept at the time that an oath, even made in error, could not be broken.

To placate their people, the Israelite chieftains told them that the Gibeonites would become "hewers of wood and drawers of water for the whole community" (Josh. 9:21). A perplexed Joshua then summoned the Gibeonites and asked them:

Why did you deceive us and tell us you lived very far from us, when in

fact you live among us? Therefore, be accursed! Never shall your descendants cease to be slaves, hewers of wood and drawers of water for the House of my God. (Josh. 9:22-23)

In what must stand as one of the most brutally candid admissions in the Bible, the Gibeonites replied to Joshua:

You see, your servants had heard that the LORD your God had promised His servant Moses to give you the whole land and to wipe out all the inhabitants of the country on your account; so we were in great fear for our lives on your account. That is why we did this thing. And now we are at your mercy; do with us what you consider right and proper. (Josh. 9:24-25)

The words "right and proper" convey the hope of the Gibeonites that a just solution could be found. Indeed, making the Gibeonites slaves seems to have been more or less agreeable to both them and the Israelites, but is it not a "just agreement" in the sense used in section 6.2. To show why this is so, it is first necessary to model the game played between the Gibeonites and Joshua and the Israelites (whom henceforth I shall lump with Joshua and refer to as simply the single player "Joshua").

As depicted in the game tree of figure 6.3, the Gibeonites must ini-

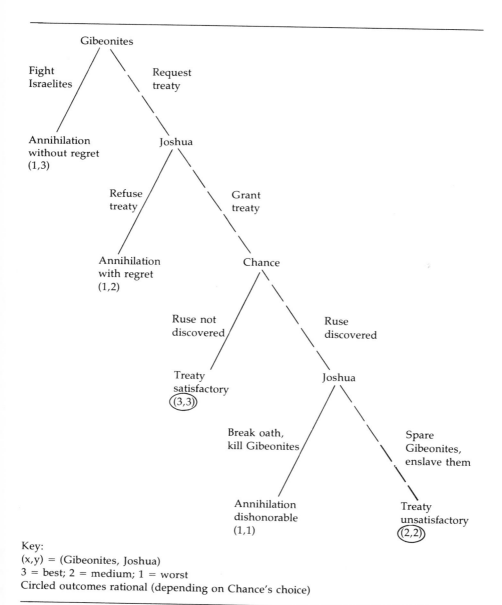

Key:
(x,y) = (Gibeonites, Joshua)
3 = best; 2 = medium; 1 = worst
Circled outcomes rational (depending on Chance's choice)

Figure 6.3 Game tree of Joshua's deception by the Gibeonites

tially choose between fighting the Israelites or seeking a peace treaty through misrepresentation of their situation. Assuming they seek a treaty, Joshua may either grant or refuse their request.

If Joshua grants the Gibeonites their request, a new "player," not modeled before, enters the picture. This player, which I call Chance, is not of course a real player capable of making rational choices with respect to a set of preferences. Rather, Chance determines whether or not the ruse of the Gibeonites is discovered, which I assume to be an event that has a nonzero probability of occurrence.

Chance becomes "known" to Joshua only when the ruse of the Gibeonites is discovered. When this occurs, Joshua has the choice of breaking the oath he made to the Gibeonites or sticking to his word. If he chooses the latter course of action, he can enslave the Gibeonites but not kill them.

For both the Gibeonites and Joshua, I postulate a three-tier ranking of outcomes: best (3), medium (2), and worst (1). Starting with the Gibeonites, I assume their worst outcome (1) occurs when any one of the following three possibilities arises: they fight the Israelites; Joshua refuses them the treaty; or they are killed by the Israelites after their ruse is discovered. Since the Gibeonites would be annihilated in

all three cases, I rate them as equally bad. Better for them would be to be spared after their ruse is discovered (2), and best would be not to have their ruse discovered at all (3)—if, indeed, this were possible.[1]

By comparison, Joshua would least like to break his sacred oath and kill the Gibeonites after their ruse is discovered (1). He would prefer to spare the Gibeonites or to have refused them a treaty in the first place (2).

I rank the latter outcome for Joshua not as high as fighting the Gibeonites at the outset (3), because—in the absence of a request for a treaty—he could not be accused of turning down a reasonable proposal from a distant and non-threatening people. Somewhat paradoxically, perhaps, I would argue that Joshua would also enjoy his best outcome (3) if the ruse were not discovered, because at least he could not be the wiser for having been deceived. (I implicitly assume that Joshua would prefer not to have his reputation sullied by having been duped.) Unfortunately for Joshua, Chance permitted him only three days before he learned of the hoax that had been perpetrated on him.

In fact, the Bible hints, if Joshua had been a little more respectful of God, he would not have suffered this hoax:

The men took [the Gibeonites' word] because of their provisions, and did not inquire of the LORD. (Josh. 9:14)

Thus, one might plausibly interpret Chance to be God, who, when ignored by Joshua and his men, lets the pact be consummated before unmasking the true origins of the Gibeonites. God, in other words, might be regarded as a player hiding behind Chance; unlike Chance, which has no preferences, God wants Joshua and the Israelites to pay a price for not consulting Him on the matter of the Gibeonites. After paying this price, Joshua appeared to show more respect by making the Gibeonites slaves "for the community and for the altar of the LORD, in the place that He would choose" (Josh. 9:27).

Whether or not Chance is controlled by God, after the discovery of the hoax the only rational course of action for Joshua was to spare the Gibeonites. I presume that he could take some solace from knowing that they would be slaves to the Israelites. Nevertheless, I rate the payoffs associated with this outcome [(2,2)] unequivocally worse for both players than the payoffs associated with a successful cover-up of the hoax [(3,3)].

Because of the intervention of Chance (or God), the rational outcome, at least for the human players, of (3,3) was not selected in this deception game. It is worth noting that if the game had terminated just prior to Chance's move, and this move were replaced by the (3,3) outcome ("ruse not discovered"), it could then be said that Joshua and the Israelites acted rationally by granting the treaty. This is the truncated game Joshua probably perceived.

But Chance did intervene to upset the calculations of Joshua. In so doing, it rendered the agreement he had made with the Gibeonites unjust, for the (2,2) outcome that occurred is unstable vis-à-vis the possibility of the (3,3) outcome.

Because the Gibeonites knew that their ruse might be discovered, they were not despondent about attaining a "2" outcome and thereby avoiding annihilation. Joshua, on the other hand, had more reason to regret Chance's choice, but it is probably unfair to blame just Chance in the selection of the (2,2) outcome. After all, it was the Gibeonites' deception that gave Chance its move, so they also must share the blame for an unjust agreement. Even Joshua does not seem totally blameless, for he did not take the necessary precautions to check up on the authenticity of the Gibeonites' claims. Like Isaac, who refused to believe that "Esau" (Jacob) was an impersonator, Joshua's gullibility—and perhaps disregard of God—came back to haunt him.

Whoever deserves the blame for Joshua's deception, a treaty was agreed to that I presume would not have been if all parties had been fully aware of moves in the game tree. Since the game that was played was one of incomplete information—at least for Joshua—it is only after the fact that his acquiescence to the Gibeonites' request renders the agreement unjust.

Had Joshua acted on his suspicions, or after consulting God, the "unjustness" of the agreement would have been evident, and he could have turned down the request of the Gibeonites for good reasons. Effectively, his "good reasons" would have transformed the (1,2) payoff for refusing their request into a (1,3) payoff; rationality considerations would then dictate that he refuse the Gibeonite request, for he would thereby obtain his best outcome (3).

This is not, of course, how Joshua saw things. Since his suspicions were not sufficiently aroused, he permitted the elusive player I have called Chance (perhaps an impersonation of God) a move. Although Joshua and the chieftains were hurt by its move—the Bible says that the Israelites "muttered against the chieftains" (Josh. 9:18) after the Gibeonite deception was discovered—both players seemed content to live with the treaty afterward. The Gibeonites walked away with their

lives, and Joshua and the Israelites had slaves to serve them; so the treaty was not such a bad bargain after all.

6.4 Solomon's Wisdom

Most of the "wisdom" of the Bible is simply asserted, as in Proverbs, which is filled with advice about proper behavior, admonitions against improper behavior, and miscellaneous sayings and aphorisms meant to be instructive on various matters. Lessons, of course, are meant to be learned from the stories of conflict and intrigue I have already discussed, but the message in these stories is usually less direct and more often subject to different interpretations.

It is a rare story, indeed, that imbues a character other than God—or one with God at his side—with a soaring intelligence and depth of insight that seem to surpass human bounds. True, most characters act rationally according to their preferences, and a few like Cain, and Moses in his later years, show by the arguments they present to God that they are brilliant strategists. It is hard, however, to find human characters who, when pitted against fellow mortals, emerge as larger-than-life figures by virtue of their godlike wisdom.

The biblical character in the Old Testament who stands out as the striking exception to this statement is Solomon, who ruled as king of Israel after David (some of whose exploits will be told in chapters 7 and 8). What is usually considered his most breathtaking judgment is described in just twelve verses in chapter 3 of the First Book of Kings.

This judgment concerns the disposition of a baby for whom two women claimed maternity. I shall model this judgment as a game Solomon devised to test the veracity of the two women's claims. Although the game as played involved one woman's moving first, Solomon could have set the rules differently—to allow for simultaneous moves—and still have achieved the same result. Also, I shall show how the concept of "wise arbitration"— to complement the notion of a "just agreement" defined earlier—can be derived from Solomon's game. Unlike a just agreement, which depends only on the choices that the parties to an agreement make, wise arbitration depends also on the choices of a nonplayer, who arbitrates a settlement between the parties to a dispute.

Solomon's game arises from a dispute between two prostitutes who come before him:

The first woman said, "Please, my lord! This woman and I live in the same house; and I gave birth to a child while she was in the house. On the third day after I was delivered, this woman also gave birth to a child. We were alone; there was no one else with us in the house, just the two of us in the house. During the night this woman's child died, because she lay on it. She arose in the night and took my son from my side while your maidservant was asleep, and laid him in her bosom; and she laid her dead son in my bosom. When I arose in the morning to nurse my son, there he was, dead; but when I looked at him closely in the morning, it was not the son I had borne." (1 Kgs. 3:17–21)

The other prostitute protested this version of their encounter:

No; the live one is my son, and the dead one is yours! (1 Kgs. 3:22)

The two women continued arguing in Solomon's presence, while he reflected:

"One says, 'This is my child, the live one, and the dead one is yours'; and the other says, 'No, the dead boy is yours, mine is the live one.'" So the king gave the order, "Fetch me a sword." (1 Kgs. 3:23–24)

Solomon's solution was one of dazzling simplicity:

Cut the live child in two, and give half to one and half to the other. (1 Kgs. 3:25)

The subtlety underlying this solution soon became apparent in the reactions of the two claimants:

But the woman whose son was the live one pleaded with the king, for she was overcome with compassion for her son. "Please, my lord," she cried, "give her the live child; only don't kill it!" The other insisted, "It shall be neither yours nor mine; cut it in two!" (1 Kgs. 3:26)

Then Solomon pronounced judgment:

"Give the live child to her [the first woman]," he said, "and do not put it to death; she is its mother." (1 Kgs. 3:27)

The story concludes with the following observation:

When all Israel heard the decision that the king had rendered, they stood in awe of the king; for they saw that he possessed divine wisdom to execute justice. (1 Kgs. 3:28)

Thus is Solomon venerated for his exemplary judgment.

The outcome matrix for the game played between the two women, reacting to Solomon's order to cut the baby in two, is shown in figure 6.4. I assume the mother's goal is to save her baby, the impostor's to win Solomon's favor; by acceding to Solomon's judgment, the impostor indicated absolutely no interest in the baby's welfare, much less having him for herself.

More specifically, the mother, I believe, would consider the best outcome (4) to be that in which both women protest Solomon's order, because their combined protest would be most likely to save the baby. If the mother protested alone, the baby perhaps might be saved, so this would be the mother's next-best outcome (3).

This latter strategy would lead to the impostor's best outcome (4); she would win Solomon's favor, because the mother's single protest would unequivocally distinguish her (the impostor's) support of the king's order and the mother's non-support. The outcome the impostor would next most prefer (3) is that in which neither she nor the mother protested the king's order, because then, although she would not be singled out favorably, she would not be in his disfavor. For the mother, though, this strategy would lead to her worst outcome (1), for the baby would surely die.

I assume that a better outcome (2) for the mother is for her not to protest and the impostor to protest; the baby might be saved, but he would not go to her. In fact, I believe, the mother would be abject for rejecting her baby when the imposter did not, though the possibil-

	Impostor	
	Protest order (P)	Don't protest order (P̄)
Mother Protest order (P)	Baby surely saved (4,2)	Baby perhaps saved; impostor wins favor of Solomon (3, 4)
Don't protest order (P̄)	Baby perhaps saved; if so, impostor gets him (2,1)	Baby surely killed (1,3)

Key:
(x,y) = (Mother, Impostor)
4 = best; 3 = next best; 2 = next worst; 1 = worst

Figure 6.4 Outcome matrix of Solomon's game

ity that the baby might survive under these circumstances prevents this outcome from being her worst. For the impostor, on the other hand, this would be an odious outcome (1), because she would lose the favor of the king by protesting his order while the mother did not. As I previously indicated, the impostor would most prefer that the opposite happen.

The actual game played was one in which the mother, by protesting the king's order, committed herself first; then the impostor responded. The payoff matrix for this 2 × 4 game is given in figure 6.5 and shows both women to have dominant strategies: the mother protests (P), and the impostor doesn't protest regardless (P̄/P̄), which leads to

outcome (3,4), the next-best outcome for the mother and the best for the impostor.

In pursuit of the truth, fortunately, Solomon had foreseen the women's true preferences. He correctly gauged that the women would play the game as I have modeled it: the mother's highest priority would be saving her baby, even at the cost of losing him to the impostor. Thus, Solomon was playing a kind of game with the women in which he read the strategies they chose in the game he devised as evidence of who was telling the truth, which is in the end what he was interested in uncovering.

Wise arbitration involves the setup of a game by an arbitrator in such a way as to distinguish truth-

		P/P	P̄/P̄	P/P̄	P̄/P	
	P	(4,2)	(3,4)	(4,2)	(3,4)	← Protest dominant
Mother	P̄	(2,1)	(1,3)	(1,3)	(2,1)	

Impostor

↑
Don't protest regardless dominant

Key:
(x,y) = (Mother, Impostor)
4 = best; 3 = next best; 2 = next worst; 1 = worst
Circled outcome rational

Figure 6.5 Payoff matrix of Solomon's game

ful from untruthful disputants. That is, the arbitrator designs the rules of the game such that play of the game reveals which player is the deceiver (assuming one disputant's claim is truthful and the other's is not). Such arbitration is "wise" in the sense that it distinguishes honest players from dishonest players by eliciting responses that, when properly interpreted, indicate who is lying and who is truthful.

It is difficult to define "properly interpreted," but one necessary condition is that the players not know the arbitrator's interpretation of their strategy choices. If they did, then presumably the players would play a different game from that which the arbitrator intends, and he thereby would not elicit the truth-revealing responses he wants.

For example, assume that the im-

postor knew that Solomon did not desire her affirmation of his order but instead intended to favor the woman (women) who protested his order. Then it would obviously be in her interest also to protest, and the game would not distinguish her from the mother.

The arbitrator does, of course, want the disputants to play a game, but the structure of their preferences should not be such that one player has to anticipate the other's choice in order to make a rational choice himself. This point can be illustrated in Solomon's game by noting that because each woman had a dominant strategy in figure 6.5, it was unnecessary for either to try to predict the other's choice. Whatever the other's choice, each woman's dominant strategy was best against it.

It is easy to show that a slight alteration in the rules of the game would still have elicited truth-revealing responses from the two women. If the women had been in separate rooms when Solomon informed each of his order, they would have played the game shown in figure 6.4, for neither woman would have been responding to the strategy choice of the other. That is, because each's strategy choice would have been made in ignorance of the other woman's choice, the game can be modeled as a 2 × 2 game.

In the 2 × 2 game shown in figure 6.4, both women have dominant strategies—the impostor to agree with the king, the mother to protest. Thus, this game, as well as the 2 × 4 game actually played—in which the mother reacted to the king's order first and the impostor knew her response—would also have ferreted out the truth.

To carry this kind of analysis one step further, consider a hypothetical game in which the impostor's preferences are the same as the mother's: both most prefer a double protest [(4,4)] and least prefer no protest [(1,1)]; each would next most prefer to protest (3) when the other does not (2). Notice in this new game that the impostor no longer has a dominant strategy of agreeing with the king; instead, she has, like the mother, a domi-

nant strategy of protesting, thus assuring the mutually best outcome of (4,4).

This game, however, is not one involving deception but rather one in which information about maternity is fugitive. Naturally, if both women have maternalistic preferences, and each protests the order, it would not make things easy for a Solomon. But well it should not, for if each woman truly believes she is the mother, and the maternity of the baby cannot be determined from any external evidence, wise arbitration alone will not be sufficient to settle the dispute. No game to ferret out the truth can be constructed, even by a Solomon, if the truth is not there to be ferreted out!

6.5 Conclusions

It is probably no accident that the stories that seem to shed the most light on justice and wisdom in the Old Testament involve deception: Rahab deceives her king by sheltering the Israelite spies and facilitating their escape; the Gibeonites deceive Joshua into believing that they have journeyed from a distant land; and one of the prostitutes attempts to deceive Solomon that a baby is hers.

It is the element of deception in each of these stories that forces the characters to make difficult strategic choices and ethical decisions:

1. Should the spies sheltered by Rahab trust a prostitute who was willing to lie to her king? They do, but they make Rahab, who must show her good faith first, painfully aware that her fate is tied to theirs. This mutual understanding renders her betrayal irrational and thereby makes the agreement they reach just.

2. Should Joshua believe the Gibeonites' tale and accept at face value the evidence they show him of their long journey? He does so despite his suspicions, granting them a peace treaty, only to learn three days later of his foolishness. The treaty is unjust precisely because Chance (or God) rendered it unstable with respect to the alternative Joshua did not consider—fighting the Gibeonites—when he put aside his suspicions and failed to consult God.

3. Should Solomon carry out his order to cut the disputed baby in two? His wisdom and perspicacity shine through when he evaluates the responses of the prostitutes to his order, based on the game he surmised they would play, and retracts it, awarding the baby to the protesting mother. The lesson seems to be that an arbitrator is wise if he deceives those whose dispute he is arbitrating in such a way as to reveal which disputant is being truthful.

These decisions raise an interesting ethical question: Can deception be put to the service of justice and wisdom? A just agreement was consummated between Rahab and the Israelite spies because she deceived her king, and Solomon's decision is applauded because he hoodwinked the impostor into thinking that he was looking for affirmation of his order. Even the Gibeonites can be admired for their strategic acumen, though they foisted upon an innocent and insufficiently God-fearing Joshua an unjust agreement.

These stories raise difficult philosophical issues concerning the morality of deception, particularly when it is ostensibly linked to just agreements or wise arbitration. As I noted, Solomon's probity has been universally extolled, but one can well imagine ingenious arbitration games that elicit only half-truths, or do not place the elicited information in a proper context.[2]

Rules of law are supposed to prevent this, but they are of course not perfect. Unscrupulous individuals, without the judicious temperament of a Solomon, may succeed in sabotaging agreements or subverting institutions. Biblical stories teach us that such problems are ameliorated by having a good knowledge of, and healthy respect for, the strategic weaknesses in situations.

Morality is empty without safeguards to enforce it, as Joshua learned to his dismay. These safe-guards may be either explicit, as were those agreed to by Rahab and the spies, or implicit in the nature of the game played, as those in the game played between the prosti-tutes who were not sophisticated enough to see through Solomon's motives. I judge arbitration schemes like Solomon's dangerous, however, because their assumption of a naïveté on the part of the play-ers may sometimes be unwar-ranted.

7 Royal Conflict

7.1 Introduction

As players in the biblical games in the Old Testament, royalty—kings and queens and the like—can be found in the Bible beginning with the First Book of Samuel. The three major Israelite kings in the Old Testament are Saul, David, and Solomon (whom I introduced in the previous chapter as both a king and an uncommonly wise man). In this chapter, I shall discuss the reign of Saul at some length, including his struggle with David, and in chapter 8 I shall discuss a different episode from David's life.

I shall also tell the story of a non-Israelite king in this chapter, whose court was filled with intrigue. The relationship that this king had with his second queen, Esther, will be the focus of analysis here. Since how this relationship developed determined in large part the outcome of a power struggle Esther had with her main antagonist for royal favors, Haman, I consider their conflict to be a "royal" one. On the other hand, the king's earlier struggle with his first queen, Vashti, I consider less to reflect royal prerogatives than a battle between the sexes. Accordingly, I analyze it in chapter 8.

Very little probably distinguishes royal conflict in any significant way from other forms of conflict and intrigue discussed in this book. Saul's muted conflict with God and Samuel in the beginning of his reign, for example, seems mostly a product of the seething jealousy his antagonists felt toward him. This emotion seems more akin to the jealousy that provoked Cain to murder Abel when he, like God and Samuel, was rejected than any peculiarly royal emotion.

If royal conflict is different from other forms of conflict, it is probably so in the a priori legitimacy royalty usually enjoys. Hence, one would expect royalty to enter most conflicts with certain advantages that make them more powerful game players. As Saul's troubles demonstrate, however, this built-in advantage is consequential only when God is *not* in the opposition.

7.2 Saul's Tenuous Position

With the conquest and settlement of Canaan largely completed, Samuel became the first prophet and judge of Israel. When the elders of Israel asked him to "appoint a king for us, to govern us like all other nations" (1 Sam. 8:5), Samuel was indignant. So was God, who told Samuel:

Heed the demand of the people in everything they say to you. For it is not you that they have rejected; it is Me they have rejected as their king. Like everything else they have done ever since I brought them out of Egypt to this day—forsaking Me and worshipping other gods—so they are doing to you. Heed their demand; but warn them solemnly, and tell them about the practices of any king who will rule over them. (1 Sam. 8:7–9)

Samuel duly warned the people that the king for whom they importuned him would conscript their sons, take their daughters as "perfumers, cooks, and bakers" (1 Sam. 8:13), seize their choice fields, vineyards, and olive groves and give them to his courtiers, and expropriate a tenth of their grain and vintage. Worst,

you shall become his slaves. The day will come when you cry out because of the king whom you yourselves have chosen; and the LORD will not answer you on that day. (1 Sam. 8:17–18)

But the people refused to listen:

"No," they said. "We must have a king over us, that we may be like all the other nations: Let our king rule over us and go out at our head and fight our battles." (1 Sam. 8:19–20)

So God grudgingly told Samuel, "Heed their demands and appoint a king for them" (1 Sam. 8:22).

At God's behest, Samuel appointed Saul ruler over the people of Israel, instructing him to

go down to Gilgal ahead of me, and I will come down to you to present burnt offerings and offer sacrifices of well-being. Wait seven days until I come to you and instruct you what you are to do next. (1 Sam. 10:8)

But Samuel did not arrive after seven days, and "the people began to scatter" (1 Sam. 13:8). To stem their sedition, Saul offered a sacrifice and, just as he had finished, Samuel arrived and rebuked him severely:

"What have you done?" Saul replied, "I saw the people leaving me and scattering; you had not come at the appointed time, and the Philistines had gathered at Michmas. I thought the Philistines would march down against me at Gilgal before I had entreated the LORD." (1 Sam. 13:11–12)

But this answer was unsatisfactory for Samuel, who prefigured God's later displeasure and estrangement:

You acted foolishly in not keeping the commandments that the LORD your God laid upon you! Otherwise the LORD would have established your dynasty over Israel forever. But now your dynasty will not endure. The LORD will seek out a man after His own heart, and the LORD will ap-

point him ruler over His people, because you did not abide by what the LORD had commanded you. (1 Sam. 13:13–14)

With his end thus foretold, it becomes clear that Saul has been set up as a fall guy—though previously he had been judged to be the best man for the kingship,

an excellent young man; no one among the Israelites was handsomer than he; he was a head taller than any of the people. (1 Sam. 9:2)

But despite these impressive physical attributes of Saul, God could simply not get over the ingratitude of the people. After He had anointed Saul as king, Samuel related God's word, adding his own reprise:

"I brought Israel out of Egypt, and I delivered you from the hands of the Egyptians and of all the kingdoms that oppressed you." But today you have rejected your God who delivered you from all your troubles and calamities. For you said, "No, set up a king over us!" (1 Sam. 10:18–19)

Chastened, finally, by God's enmity, the people beseeched Samuel:

Intercede for your servants with the LORD your God that we may not die, for we have added to all our sins the wickedness of asking for a king. (1 Sam. 12:19)

Samuel offered the people a reassuring response but concluded with a warning that "if you persist in your wrongdoing, both you and your king shall be swept away" (1 Sam. 12:25).

What makes Saul's case even more pathetic is that he never sought the kingship. He was, by his own self-deprecating testimony,

only a Benjamite, from the smallest of the tribes of Israel, and my clan is the least of all the clans of the tribe of Benjamin! (1 Sam. 9:21)

Previously Samuel had told him that all Israel wanted him. After Saul's disclaimer about his qualifications, he asked, incredulously, "Why do you [Samuel] say such things to me?" (1 Sam. 9:21)

God did help Saul and the Israelites win victories over the Ammonites and the Philistines. Yet, in addition to the disturbing signs of Saul's eventual ruination alluded to earlier, God held something back. For example, when Saul inquired of God whether to pursue the fleeing Philistines after defeating them in battle, he received no answer.

Saul, on the other hand, held nothing back. He made Herculean efforts to pay homage to God, even offering to sacrifice his own son,

Jonathan, for breaking a fast he had ordered. But Jonathan, who admitted to the slight impropriety of having "tasted a bit of honey with the tip of the stick in my hand" (1 Sam. 14:43), was saved by the remonstrations of the people.

God, ambivalent up to now about the man whom He had reluctantly invested as king, eventually paved the way for his undoing and final degradation. Samuel, a willing accomplice, related to Saul God's word:

I am exacting the penalty for what Amalek did to Israel, for the assault he made upon them on the road, on their way up from Egypt. Now go, attack Amalek, and proscribe all that belongs to him. Spare no one, but kill alike men and women, infants and sucklings, oxen and sheep, camels and asses. (1 Sam. 15:2–3)

A rather harsh edict, especially as several generations had passed since the Israelites had fled Egypt. But God was not known for having a short memory, especially on matters that He took to be personal affronts.

Saul dutifully carried out this savage edict, except to take alive Agag, king of the Amalekites, and spare

the best of the sheep, the oxen, the second born, the lambs, and all else that was of value. They would not proscribe them; they proscribed only what was cheap and worthless. (1 Sam. 15:9)

This sounds like a sensible calculation, except that it contravened God's unsparing edict, causing God to "regret that I made Saul king, for he has turned away from Me and has not carried out My commands" (1 Sam. 15:11).

Samuel, whose relations with Saul had never been smooth, was angry, too. His anger was exacerbated when he was told that Saul had set up a monument to himself. To make things even worse, Saul showed no remorse when he greeted Samuel and said he had obeyed God's command. Samuel vehemently disputed this claim, pointing to the sheep and oxen Saul had taken, but Saul retorted that these animals were saved to be given as a sacrifice to God.

Tenaciously the two men fought back and forth on this issue until Samuel was driven to make God's desires unmistakably clear:

Does the LORD delight in burnt offerings and sacrifices
As much as in obedience to the LORD's command?
Surely, obedience is better than sacrifice,
Compliance than the fat of rams. (1 Sam. 15:22)

Saul, suddenly penitent, then admitted to having sinned because "I was afraid of the troops and I yielded to them" (1 Sam. 15:24).

As I see it, the game God/Samuel played against Saul was an unfair one from the start. Saul was, as it were, plucked from nowhere and set up as king, much as Moses earlier was catapulted into the position of leader of the Israelites (section 5.2). But there is a crucial difference between these figures: God was willing to give Moses practically all the help he wanted, including a brother who stood at his side and spoke his lines for him; Saul, on the other hand, received much less help from God, who apparently was very upset that His chosen people would so much as wish for a king, much less demand one. Feeling utterly dejected by such inconsiderateness, God found Saul an obvious target on whom to vent his anger.

Because of their strained relationship, Samuel was not much help to Saul, either, though Samuel's role as judge should have made him an ideal coach to a neophyte king. However, Samuel had his own grudge to bear: his sons had been rejected by the elders of Israel even though, in his old age, Samuel had opportunistically tried to appoint them as judges to replace him. The elders had told Samuel simply that his sons "have not followed your

[Samuel's] ways" (1 Sam. 8:5), but the Bible also reports that the sons "were bent on gain, they accepted bribes, and they subverted justice" (1 Sam. 8:3).

It is certainly not surprising that a dejected God and his embittered sycophant, Samuel, would lash out at a hapless Saul. What is surprising, perhaps, is that they kept their vendetta muted at first, and mostly used innuendos. They even went through the motions of supporting the king they could not stand, lest they be accused of reneging on their commitment to respect the people's desire.

In fact, it is "the people," unwittingly, who probably play the most significant role in Saul's rise and fall. When they impertinently cry out for a king, God reluctantly accedes to their wish; when they recant—partially to appease God—He seizes upon their reversion. Whether God in these instances is a democrat or a fawning autocrat, I hesitate to say.

For all the vaunted respect the people receive, they do not give very substantial reasons for their initial wish—just a desire to be like everybody else, with a king to lead them in battles. No wonder God felt resentment that His chosen people were not being very discriminating about their leadership preferences!

But when the people admit to having gone too far in their request for a king, and evince a willingness to retract it, God and Samuel are ready to step in and engineer Saul's fall from favor. Saul's failure to carry out to the letter God's command to eviscerate the Amalekites in a horrific slaughter is just the excuse Samuel needs to justify an end to Saul's reign:

Because you rejected the LORD's command,
He has rejected you as king. (1 Sam. 15:23)

Why did not Saul strictly obey God's command? Once Saul had learned from Samuel that God was no longer on his side (1 Sam. 13:13–14), he may have decided he had no alternative but to fend for himself—and to listen to the people (1 Sam. 15:24) at least as much as to God. In this manner, God's abandonment of Saul may have diminished Saul's faith, which in turn triggered his disobedience and eventual downfall, thereby fulfilling Samuel's earlier prophecy.

The final rupture between Saul and God is echoed, symbolically, in the parting scene between Samuel and Saul:

As Samuel turned to leave, Saul seized the corner of his robe, and it tore. And Samuel said to him, "The

LORD has this day torn the kingship over Israel away from you and has given it to another who is worthier than you. Moreover, the Glory of Israel does not deceive or change His mind, for He is not human that He should change His mind." (1 Sam. 15:27–29)

In my opinion, Samuel's statement just does not square with the facts of Saul's reign and the events that preceded it. God *did* change His mind about a king when the people clamored for one. Also, once Saul was installed, the divine support he had received quickly evaporated. When the people themselves had second thoughts about having a king, God was more than willing to escalate innuendos into a complete reversal of His original position. Although Saul certainly showed signs of weakness in deferring to the people and not strictly obeying God's commands, his castigation by God/Samuel has devious undertones that smack of a frame-up.

God and Samuel's actions in this sordid affair are, I think, entirely consistent with their motives, which essentially involve avenging the insult the people handed to them by demanding a king. (Why the people are not punished directly for their apostasy is not clear, but presumably God/Samuel find it easier to vent their anger on the living embodiment of their displea-

sure.) Buffeted by their increasingly aggressive and duplicitous tactics, the luckless Saul becomes a quite helpless pawn, and his kingship turns sour.

I find it hard not to feel sympathy for Saul as he tries to stave off defeat in an unfair game against inimical forces beyond his control. One should not overlook the fact, however, that if God and Samuel behave ignominiously in this affair, the fickle people collectively stand behind them, influencing their choices as well as Saul's. They are the significant behind-the-scenes player in this sad story.

7.3 Conflict with David

It would be nice to say that Saul's plight ends with his rejection by God. But it does not, for God is not content just to abandon Saul; it is also reported that "an evil spirit from the LORD began to terrify him [Saul]" (1 Sam. 16:14).

To dispel this spirit, Saul's servants located "a stalwart fellow and a warrior, sensible in speech, and handsome in appearance" (1 Sam. 16:18). His name was David; by playing the lyre, he gave Saul relief. Saul came to love David and made him one of his arms-bearers.

David soon gained fame by slaying the Philistine giant Goliath. After his victory, he succeeded so well in every venture he undertook for Saul that Saul put him in command of all his soldiers.

Further distinction was heaped upon David after he slaughtered great numbers of Philistines. In fact, on his homecoming with the army, women, dancing, greeted David's success with the contumacious ditty:

Saul has slain his thousands;
David, his tens of thousands!
(1 Sam. 18:7)

The envy directed by God and Samuel against Saul earlier was now turned by Saul against the rising new star in his kingdom:

Saul was much distressed and greatly vexed about the matter. For he said, "To David they have given tens of thousands, and to me they have given thousands. All that he lacks is the kingship!" From that day on Saul kept a jealous eye on David. (1 Sam. 18:8–9)

When God's evil spirit gripped Saul again, he could contain himself no longer and hurled a spear at David, who was trying to soothe him by playing the lyre. David twice swerved from the spear meant to pin him against the wall, which agitated Saul further, for he saw this as a sign that God had indeed forsaken him. To keep David at bay, he removed him from his household and gave him the command of

a thousand men. David "was successful in all his undertakings, for the LORD was with him" (1 Sam. 18:14).

The portents were now unmistakable. With David's star still ascending in the eyes of the people, Saul next offered to give his eldest daughter in marriage to David if he would pledge to fight the Philistines. This plan fell through, but when Saul's other daughter, Michal, fell in love with David, Saul realized that her marriage to David would also suit his plans:

I will give her to him, and she can serve as a snare for him, so that the Philistines may kill him. (1 Sam. 18:21)

But David did not die; in fact, he more than paid the bride price of one hundred foreskins of Philistines by killing two hundred of them. As a consequence, Saul "grew still more afraid of David; and Saul was David's enemy ever after" (1 Sam. 18:29). The fissure, it seems, had become irreparable.

Saul's fear soon took on more menacing overtones:

Saul urged his son Jonathan and all his courtiers to kill David. But Saul's son Jonathan was very fond of David, and Jonathan told David, "My father Saul is bent on killing you." (1 Sam. 19:1–2)

Bravely, Jonathan reproached his father for his evil intentions, reminding him that David had never wronged him but instead had put his life on the line against the Philistines. Chastened by Jonathan's arguments, Saul demurred and welcomed David back to his household.

But God's evil spirit returned to Saul, and he again unsuccessfully tried to impale David on his spear. After David eluded him, he fled, and Saul plotted once more to kill him. But David's wife, Michal, foiled her father's plan by letting David down from a window of their home and putting a dummy figure in his bed. Then Saul caustically asked Michal:

Why did you play that trick on me and let my enemy get away safely?" "Because," Michal answered Saul, "he said to me: 'Help me get away or I'll kill you.'" (1 Sam. 19:17)

This was a lie, for it had actually been Michal who had persuaded David to flee. While loyal to David, Michal was not as honest with her father as her brother, Jonathan, had been.

David had several more close calls with Saul. He was aided as a fugitive by the prophet Samuel, Saul's old antagonist, in one set of encounters, by Jonathan in others.

Indeed, Jonathan's loyalty to David, whom he loved "as himself" (1 Sam. 18:1), forced Jonathan into a break with his father in an acrimonious and tumultuous exchange filled with obloquy:

Saul flew into a rage against Jonathan. "You son of a perverse, rebellious woman! . . . Have him [David] brought to me, for he is marked for death." But Jonathan spoke up and said to his father, "Why should he be put to death? What has he done?" At that, Saul threw his spear at him to strike him down; and Jonathan realized that his father was determined to do away with David. Jonathan rose from the table in a rage. (1 Sam. 20:30-34)

The scene was also charged with emotion when Jonathan next saw David:

They kissed each other and wept together; David wept the longer. (1 Sam. 20:41)

Unlike the family conflicts discussed in chapter 3, the vitriolic conflict between Saul and Jonathan, involving as it did David, transcended their immediate family.

In time, David organized a band of men and had to fend for himself in the wilderness, fighting the Philistines at the same time that he tried

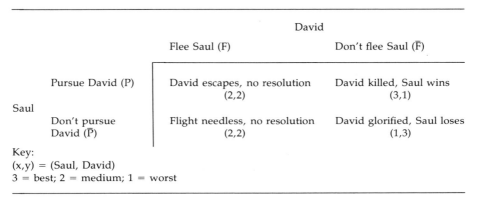

		David	
		Flee Saul (F)	Don't flee Saul (F̄)
Saul	Pursue David (P)	David escapes, no resolution (2,2)	David killed, Saul wins (3,1)
	Don't pursue David (P̄)	Flight needless, no resolution (2,2)	David glorified, Saul loses (1,3)

Key:
(x,y) = (Saul, David)
3 = best; 2 = medium; 1 = worst

Figure 7.1 Outcome matrix for flight of David

to elude Saul. During this time, he conspired with Jonathan, who exhorted him:

"Do not be afraid: the hand of my father will never touch you. You are going to be king over Israel and I shall be second to you; and even my father Saul knows this is so." And the two of them entered into a pact before the LORD. (1 Sam. 23:17–18)

It thus seems that Jonathan's hopes for future rank as well as friendship underlay his support of David.

The pursuit of David by Saul up to this point can be modeled as a game of total conflict (see section 2.4) in which each player has two strategies. Saul may or may not pursue David, who must choose between fleeing or not fleeing Saul,

as shown in the outcome matrix of figure 7.1.

On a three-point scale, I assume David's two outcomes associated with fleeing Saul are medium (2) for both players. This is so because, given that David eludes Saul if he pursues him, and remains in exile otherwise, there is no resolution to the conflict between them. On the other hand, I assume that Saul wins (3) if David does not flee and, as a consequence, is captured (1); if Saul doesn't pursue David, and David remains in the kingdom, David is glorified (3) and Saul loses (1). Thus, the game is one in which there is either a winner and a loser, or no resolution to the conflict, in which case the game is repeated.

Since David's strategy choice in this game followed Saul's, their

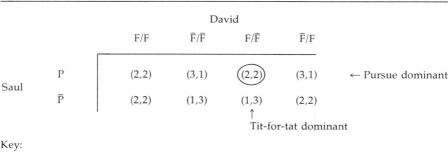

Figure 7.2 Payoff matrix for flight of David

game is properly modeled as a 2 × 4 game in which Saul chooses first. The payoff matrix for this game, shown in figure 7.2, indicates that both players had dominant strategies of pursuit (Saul) and tit-for-tat (David), resulting in the no-resolution outcome that I believe accurately describes what actually occurred in the biblical game.

The resolution of the Saul-David conflict was not far off. Saul and three thousand men, in hot pursuit of David, stopped near a cave; unbeknownst to them, David and his men sat concealed inside. A bizarre scene unfolded:

Saul went in to relieve himself. Now David and his men were sitting in the back of the cave.

David's men said to him, "This is the day of which the LORD said to

you, 'I will deliver your enemy into your hands; you can do with him as you please.'" (1 Sam. 24:4-5)

David did not let this opportunity pass him by:

David went and stealthily cut off the corner of Saul's cloak. But afterward David reproached himself for cutting off the corner of Saul's cloak. He said to his men, "The LORD forbid that I should do such a thing to my lord— the LORD's anointed—that I should raise my hand against him; for he is the LORD's anointed." David rebuked his men and did not permit them to attack Saul. (1 Sam. 24:5-8)

After Saul left the cave, David called out to him, "My lord king" (1 Sam. 24:9)! Saul looked around, and David, prostrating himself in obeisance before a startled Saul, vividly contrasted their situations:

Why do you listen to the people who say, "David is out to do you harm?" You can see for yourself now that the LORD delivered you into my hands in the cave today. And though I was urged to kill you, I showed you pity; for I said, "I will not raise a hand against my lord, since he is the LORD's anointed." Please, sir, take a close look at the corner of your cloak in my hand; for when I cut off the corner of your cloak, I did not kill you. You must see plainly that I have done nothing evil or rebellious, and I have never wronged you. Yet you are bent on taking my life. May the LORD judge between you and me! (1 Sam. 24:10-13)

Finally, David pledged, "My hand will never touch you" (1 Sam. 24:13), and Saul gratefully responded:

You are right, not I; for you have treated me generously, but I have treated you badly. Yes, you have just revealed how generously you have treated me. . . . I know now that you will become king, and that the kingship over Israel will remain in your hands. (1 Sam. 24:18-21)

Thus Saul, eclipsed by David, proved himself a gracious loser. At the same time, however, he also extracted from David an oath to spare his descendants, which makes him hardly a loser at all!

This final episode in the Saul-David conflict is best modeled, I believe, as a game of partial conflict. The game tree for this episode is shown in figure 7.3. David first must choose between killing and sparing Saul; then, having cut off a corner of Saul's cloak, he can reveal himself to Saul and show him the corner, or not; finally, Saul can admit his wrongs and ask forgiveness for his descendants or seek revenge again.

On a three-tier ranking, the best outcome for both players is clearly to bury their differences [(3,3)]. Continued conflict can occur in two ways: if David fails to reveal himself by showing Saul the piece of cloak; or if Saul, after realizing David's generosity, still persists in pursuing him. In either case, I rank the outcomes worst (1) for David, medium (2) for Saul, since the conflict remains unresolved. This is especially detrimental to David, who clearly does not want to endure a repetition of the game.

David's medium outcome would be to kill Saul (2). This would resolve the conflict, but David would murder a king he thinks should live. For Saul, of course, dying by David's sword would be his worst (1) outcome.

Working backward from Saul's

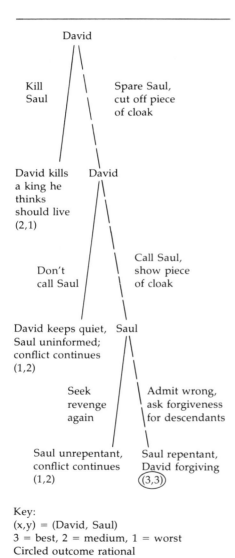

David

Kill
Saul

Spare Saul,
cut off piece
of cloak

David kills
a king he
thinks
should live
(2,1)

David

Don't
call Saul

Call Saul,
show piece
of cloak

David keeps quiet,
Saul uninformed;
conflict continues
(1,2)

Saul

Seek
revenge
again

Admit wrong,
ask forgiveness
for descendants

Saul unrepentant,
conflict continues
(1,2)

Saul repentant,
David forgiving
(3,3)

Key:
(x,y) = (David, Saul)
3 = best, 2 = medium, 1 = worst
Circled outcome rational

Figure 7.3 Game tree of Saul-David confrontation at cave

last move, his rational choice would be to admit his wrong, for (3,3) is better for him than (1,2). David, anticipating this choice, would prefer to cut off a piece of Saul's cloak and show it to him, for (3,3) is superior for him to either (1,2) or (2,1). Thus, (3,3) is the rational outcome in this game and one preferred by both players to any other outcome.

The episode I have just described in the Saul-David conflict signals an important change in the nature of the game they played. Because of David's dramatic action at the cave, in which he clearly demonstrated he had no desire to kill Saul, the game was transformed into a game of substantial agreement, with both players agreeing on the best (3) outcome. Thereby David's action produced a felicitous turn of events for the players, which neither God nor Samuel was willing—or able—to effect in the earlier game they played against Saul. Truly, the earlier game reeked of calumny and vindictiveness, but the present game exudes warmth and respect on David's part for God-invested royalty (perhaps partly motivated by a fear of God's punishment for murdering a king). The irony is that God did not place nearly so high a value on the sanctity of His royal investiture of Saul as did David.

It is perhaps somewhat puzzling that while Saul is bitterly condemned by God and Samuel, David leans over backward to show him the respect he thinks he deserves, despite Saul's many attempts on his life. Why is David so respectful, even obsequious, toward Saul? In an alternative account of the cave episode, David, finding Saul asleep in his camp, is more explicit about why he wants to spare Saul's life:

"Don't do him violence! No one can lay hands on the LORD's anointed with impunity." And David went on, "As the LORD lives, the LORD Himself will strike him down, or his time will come and he will die, or he will go down to battle and perish." (1 Sam. 26:9–10)

In fact, David's prediction is uncannily accurate, because Saul, in a battle with the Philistines in which David plays no part, is wounded by archers. Jonathan and his two other sons are killed, and Saul, in desperation, tells his arms-bearer:

Draw your sword and run me through, so that the uncircumcised may not run me through and make sport of me. (1 Sam. 31:4)

When the arms-bearer refuses, Saul, in a final heroic gesture, "grasped the sword and fell upon it" (1 Sam. 31:4).

7.4 Esther's Intercession

A quieter kind of heroism is displayed in the final story of royal conflict I shall analyze. This conflict does not involve a challenge to a king by either God or a human competitor. Rather, the conflict swirls around machinations and legerdemain in the royal court by an ambitious courtier determined to destroy his enemies.

After Ahasuerus, king of Persia, deposed Queen Vashti (their conflict is described in section 8.4), a search was made of the kingdom for a beautiful young virgin to be the new queen. Esther, who had lost both her parents and had been adopted by her uncle, Mordecai, was "shapely and beautiful" (Esther 2:7). When she was brought to King Ahasuerus, he

loved Esther more than all the other women, and she won his grace and favor more than all the virgins. So he set a royal diadem on her head and made her queen instead of Vashti. (Esther 2:17)

Now Esther was a Jew; but on Mordecai's instructions she did not disclose this fact to Ahasuerus. On the other hand, when Mordecai discovered a plot against the king, Esther not only told the king about it—resulting in the execution of the plotters—but also that Mordecai was the source of her intelligence; this "was recorded in the book of annals at the instance of the king." (Esther 2:23)

Next to appear on the scene is Haman, who had been advanced by the king to the highest position in the royal court. All bowed down and did obeisance to him except Mordecai. Incensed, Haman

disdained to lay hands on Mordecai alone; having been told who Mordecai's people were, Haman plotted to do away with all the Jews, Mordecai's people, throughout the kingdom of Ahasuerus. (Esther 3:6)

Taking his grievance to Ahasuerus, Haman turned a personal affront into a general indictment of the Jews for insubordination:

There is a certain people, scattered and dispersed among the other peoples in all the provinces of your realm, whose laws are different from those of any other people and who do not obey the king's laws; and it is not in Your Majesty's interest to tolerate them. If it please Your Majesty, let an edict be drawn for their destruction, and I will pay ten thousand talents of silver to the stewards for deposit in the royal treasury. (Esther 3:8-9)

The king declined the silver but allowed a decree to be issued that all

Jews were to be exterminated on a certain day.

There followed great mourning among the Jews. Mordecai, in a message to Esther, bade her "to go to the king and to appeal to him and to plead with him for her people" (Esther 4:8). But Esther was fearful for her life, because, as she explained to Mordecai:

All the king's courtiers and the people of the king's provinces know that, if any person, man or woman, enters the king's presence in the inner court without having been summoned, there is but one law for him—that he be put to death. Only if the king extends the golden scepter to him may he live. Now I have not been summoned to visit the king for the last thirty days. (Esther 4:11)

Mordecai scoffed that Esther should indeed be afraid, but not for the reasons she gave:

Do not imagine that you, of all the Jews, will escape with your life by being in the king's palace. On the contrary, if you keep silent in this crisis, relief and deliverance will come to the Jews from another quarter, while you and your father's house will perish. (Esther 4:13-14)

To this sardonic warning Mordecai added the suggestion that divine providence might have had a role

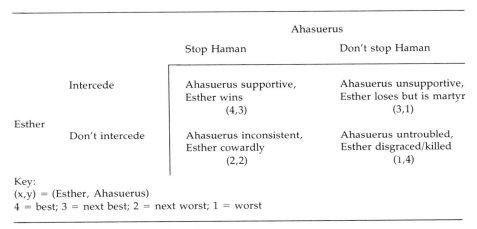

Figure 7.4 Outcome matrix of Esther's intercession

in Esther's elevation to her present royal status:

And who knows, perhaps you have attained to royal position for just such a crisis. (Esther 4:14)

Asking for spiritual assistance from her people, Esther then offered a stoic response:

Go, assemble all the Jews who live in Shushan [the capital city], and fast in my behalf; do not eat or drink for three days, night or day. I and my maidens will observe the same fast. Then I shall go to the king, though it is contrary to the law; and if I am to perish, I shall perish! (Esther 4:16)

Esther's stoicism, I submit, is not untouched by logic. Consider the outcomes of the game she played with Ahasuerus, as depicted in the outcome matrix in figure 7.4. Obviously, by interceding before the king, she was playing a risky strategy. But even if she lost and was killed by the king, she could not be faulted for not trying to save her people. Indeed, to them she would be a martyr, so I rate Esther's unsuccessful intercession next best for her (3), her best outcome of course being to intercede successfully (4).

Esther's next-worst outcome (2) would be to turn down her uncle, given that Haman were stopped, for then she would be branded a coward for not having tried to save the Jews. Her worst outcome (1) would be to allow the extermination to proceed, for she would not only be disgraced if Haman were not stopped but also could be killed herself, as Mordecai had reminded her.

I believe Ahasuerus would have been untroubled by the execution if Esther had not interceded, because he held no special brief for the Jews. Of course, if Esther's religion were made known to him, Ahasuerus would face the dismaying decision of whether to allow her to be executed or make her an exception. But this would not have concerned him when Haman was about to effect his scheme, because if Esther did not intercede, he would never be the wiser about the true state of affairs of the Jews, much less that his queen was one of them. Accordingly, I rank the status quo, in which Esther does not intercede and Ahasuerus does not countermand Haman's order, to be the king's best outcome (4)—at least before he learns of Esther's identity.

Next best (3) for Ahasuerus would be to support Esther, whom he loved, after she interceded on behalf of the Jews. Next worst (2) would be simply to cancel his order in the absence of Esther's intercession, for then the king would appear inconsistent and weak. Ahasuerus's worst (1) outcome would be not to support Esther after her intercession, because he would lose not only another queen but also the woman he loved. Thus, in a face-to-face showdown with Haman cre-

ated by Esther's intercession, Esther would win—obtain her best outcome of "4"—because "3" is better than "1" for Ahasuerus in the outcome matrix of figure 7.4.

The problem with this representation—or the 2 × 4 representation of the payoff matrix in which Esther acts first (not shown)—is that if the king refuses to extend his golden scepter to Esther, that would be the end of the game for her. Thus, it is somewhat inaccurate to give Esther the choice of interceding, because that choice is not entirely up to her.

This is the reason, I believe, that Esther asked her fellow Jews to fast for her. Once she gained an audience with the king, she did not doubt her ability to persuade him of the rightness of her cause. She did worry, though, that he might not deign to see her, might even kill her, for acting impudently.

I also think Esther worried that if she did not act, the Jews would be saved without her help, as Mordecai had predicted, in which case her procrastination would look self-serving and cowardly. Should this be the case, then effectively the second column of outcomes in figure 7.4, associated with Ahasuerus's not stopping Haman, can be deleted from the outcome matrix. That is to say, Esther had good reason to believe that Haman's plot would not succeed, even if she kept silent. Given a choice between a "4" and a "2" outcome in the first column, Esther would obviously choose her strategy—intercede—associated with the "4," thereby reaping the benefit of acting bravely and saving her people and herself.

But this calculation, like that alluded to earlier in which Esther anticipated the outcome of a face-to-face showdown with Haman, does not fully capture the complexity of Esther's choice. As I previously indicated, she could not be sure the king would even grant her an audience. After all, it had been thirty days since she had last seen Ahasuerus.

That Esther overcame her apprehensions in the end attests as much to her astute calculations as to her character. Indeed, though her assessment of the situation was correct, Esther was still very careful to be discreet about implementing her strategy:

On the third day, Esther put on royal apparel and stood in the inner court of the king's palace, facing the king's palace, while the king was sitting on his royal throne in the throne room facing the entrance of the palace. As soon as the king saw Queen Esther standing in the court, she won his favor. The king extended to Esther the golden scepter which he had in his hand, and Esther approached and touched the tip of the scepter. "What troubles you, Queen Esther?" the king

asked. "And what is your request? Even to half the kingdom, it shall be granted you." "If it please Your Majesty," Esther replied, "let Your Majesty and Haman come today to the feast that I have prepared for him." (Esther 5:1-4)

Still refusing to divulge her wishes, Esther was all indirection:

At the wine feast the king asked Esther, "What is your wish? It shall be granted you. And what is your request? Even to half the kingdom, it shall be fulfilled." "My wish," replied Esther, "my request—if Your Majesty will do me the favor, if it please Your Majesty to grant my wish and to accede to my request—let Your Majesty and Haman come to the feast which I shall prepare for them; and tomorrow I will do Your Majesty's bidding." (Esther 5:6-8)

Thus, the suspense builds as Esther lays the foundation for Haman's humiliation with drink and charm. Haman at first was pleased, then angered:

That day Haman went out happy and lighthearted. But when Haman saw Mordecai in the palace gate, and Mordecai did not rise or even stir on his account, Haman was filled with rage at him. Nevertheless, Haman controlled himself and went home. (Esther 5: 9-10)

Despite his rage at Mordecai's rudeness and arrogance, Haman bragged to his wife, Zeresh, of his invitation to Queen Esther's feast. She and Haman's friends advised him to erect a stake fifty cubits high and recommend to the king that Mordecai be impaled on it the day of the banquet.

Then, perhaps by divine intervention, a remarkable coincidence occurred. The king could not sleep, and when he ordered that the book of records be read to him, he was told that Mordecai had never been honored for saving his life from those who plotted against him.

When Haman entered the king's court the next day, the king asked:

"What should be done for a man whom the king desires to honor?" Haman said to himself, "Whom would the king desire to honor more than me?" (Esther 6:6)

Haman then answered that this man should be regally attired, with a royal diadem set on his head, and led on a horse the king had ridden through the city square, with the proclamation made:

This is what is done for the man whom the king desires to honor! (Esther 6:9)

The king then said to a stunned Haman:

Get the garb and the horse, as you have said, and do this to Mordecai the Jew, who sits in the king's gate. Omit nothing of all you have proposed. (Esther 6:10)

The end quickly approached for Haman. At the second banquet, over wine again, the king repeated his question to Esther about her wishes. Now she was finally ready to drop the bombshell:

"If Your Majesty will do me the favor, and if it pleases Your Majesty, let my life be granted as my wish, and my people at my request. For we have been sold, my people and I, to be destroyed, massacred, and exterminated. Had we only been sold as bondmen and bondwomen, I would have been silent; for the adversary is not worthy of the king's trouble."

Thereupon King Ahasuerus demanded of Queen Esther, "Who is he and where is he who dared do this?" "The adversary and enemy," replied Esther, "is this evil Haman!" (Esther 7:3-6)

The king then left the wine feast in a fury, leaving a terrified Haman to grovel for his life before Esther. When the king stalked back in, Haman had clumsily undercut his already precarious position:

Haman was lying prostrate on the couch on which Esther reclined.

"Does he mean," cried the king, "to ravish the queen in my own palace?" No sooner did these words leave the king's lips than Haman's face was covered [blanched]. Then Harbonah, one of the eunuchs in attendance on the king, said, "What is more, a stake is standing at Haman's house, fifty cubits high, which Haman made for Mordecai—the man whose words saved the king." "Impale him on it!" the king ordered. So they impaled Haman on the stake which he had put up for Mordecai, and the king's fury abated. (Esther 7:8–10)

For anyone with a sense of irony, this kind of biblical justice—being hoisted with one's own petard—is hard to rival. But as so often happens in the Bible, the matter does not end with this happy twist for the Jews. While Mordecai "was now powerful in the royal palace" (Esther 9:4), it is also reported that

the Jews struck at their enemies with the sword, slaying and destroying; they wreaked their will upon their enemies. (Esther 9:5)

Included in the slaughter were Haman's ten sons, who were impaled on the stake Haman had built.

The thick plot and heavy irony of this story are almost too astonishing to believe—and hence to model as a serious game played by rational players. I can offer no game-theoretic explanation, for example, of why Mordecai first went unrewarded for his good deed to the king, only to be remembered on the day that Haman had slated for his execution. Nor does there seem to be any underlying rationale for Mordecai's instructing Esther to withhold from Ahasuerus her identity as a Jew when she became his new queen. To be sure, the plot depends on Ahasuerus's not knowing the plight of Esther until the end, but the reason for Mordecai's secretiveness in the beginning is somewhat of a mystery.

The unexplained coincidences and adventitious events in the Esther story may, of course, result from divine intervention. God, however, is never mentioned in the Old Testament version of Esther, though the less secular Greek version of this story in the Apocrypha of the Bible makes repeated references to Him.

What is not beyond natural explanation in the Book of Esther, I contend, is Esther's decision to approach Ahasuerus. I use the word "approach," rather than "intercede," as used in the figure 7.4 outcome matrix, because Esther shrewdly waited in the wings and hoped that Ahasuerus would see her and beckon her to come before him.

This seems to me to have been a very calculated move on her part to ensure that the king would not be offended by her entry into his presence. Only after her demure entry did Esther consider when "intercession" would be appropriate and how to prepare for it.

The king seemed enchanted by both Esther and her delicate approach. (By contrast, it was Vashti's brazenness, as I shall show in section 8.4, that Ahasuerus had found unbearable in his former queen.) After receiving Esther, Ahasuerus immediately promised her up to half his kingdom, but Esther kept gently putting him off. By getting Ahasuerus to repeat his offer several times, it became almost beyond retraction when Esther finally identified the villain she wanted dispatched.

In this manner, Esther masterfully worked her feminine charm. She knew the king's preferences for a subservient queen, and she played this role to the hilt. At the core, though, I believe Esther was cunning and hard as nails, and the king, I assume, appreciated these qualities, too.

After she plied Ahasuerus with sweet talk and wine, it is hard to imagine how Esther's intercession could have failed. Indeed, I find it not inconceivable that Esther herself might have set Haman up for the king's return at the second banquet by allowing, even encouraging, him to assume a compromising position on the couch next to her.

Ahasuerus's adoring queen, then, was also a wily game player who planned her moves with great deftness. Unlike the tactless Mordecai, who insisted on continually flouting Haman, Esther demonstrated how tact could carry the day by smoothing the way for her intercession on behalf of herself and her fellow Jews. Thereby Esther asserted her independence of her uncle at the same time that she adhered to his basic precepts and followed his advice on intercession.

7.5 Conclusions

I suggested at the beginning of this chapter that there may be nothing particularly distinctive about royal conflict: human emotions are common to royalty and nonroyalty alike. I would only add here, if the lesson is not already clear, that God—at least as far as His emotions are concerned—should not be excluded from either royal or nonroyal company.

God's raging jealousy over Saul's accession to the kingship of Israel would perhaps be more understandable if He had opposed Saul from the start. But in fact Saul was handpicked by God both for his general superiority and his impressive physical attributes. These qualities, apparently, made him a real threat to both God and Samuel, whose sons had been rejected for elevation to judgeships. Significantly, when God later singled out David for succession to the throne, Samuel made a point of downgrading physical assets:

Pay no attention to his appearance or his stature, for I have rejected him. For not as man sees [does the LORD see]; man sees only what is visible, but the LORD sees into the heart. (1 Sam. 16:7)

Curiously, it is not Saul's pure heart that counts when he violates the letter but not the spirit of God's command to destroy the Amalekites.

God also felt rejected because it was the first time His chosen people had sought a king. Moreover, for them to make this request simply to ape the practice of other peoples was downright unflattering to God.

The Israelites' expressed desire for a king and, then, their second thoughts about having one, also encouraged a conspiracy by God and Samuel against Saul. If the Israelites' desires had stabilized, or if they had been less temperamental, they might have deterred, or at least inhibited, subterfuges against the new king.

Adding to Saul's woes was his own anxiety about pleasing the people. Caught in a terrible bind between their grumblings and God and Samuel's commands, his position was severely attenuated.

In his prolonged struggle with David, Saul's own jealousy surfaced. Although David tried to keep Saul's God-induced evil spirit under control, his military victories enraged Saul further. So did the rebellion of his son, Jonathan, who was torn between family loyalty and steadfast friendship to David. What is amazing to me is that out of these corrosive relationships and the resulting turmoil David, by a single (nonfatal) stroke of his sword, reconciled all conflicting parties. No wonder God favored him; perhaps He saw in him another Moses!

There is no Moses in Esther's story, nor any mean-spirited or vindictive God, either. Instead, there is the female embodiment of beauty and charm—and tact and daring as well. The exquisite use Esther makes of these qualities in a superbly choreographed *pas de deux* with Ahasuerus, and *pas de trois* with Haman as well, leaves Haman gasping. The irony of Ahasuerus's administering the fatal blow against his favorite courtier makes the plot seem even more fabulous. But as I tried to show, the underlying rationale for Esther's actions are neither hard to grasp nor incredible.

If royal conflict is distinctive, it is probably because it is more consequential than ordinary conflicts, which impinge on fewer people. That is why I think it is worth distinguishing, even if it is just another manifestation of common struggles all people have.

Conflict Between the Sexes

8.1 Introduction

All the instances of family conflict I analyzed in chapter 4 involved siblings, with the exception of the generational conflict between Joseph's brothers and their father, Jacob (section 4.4). Other instances of family conflict I have touched upon include that between two brothers, Moses and Aaron (section 5.6), a father and son, Saul and Jonathan (section 7.3), and an uncle and niece, Mordecai and Esther (section 7.4).

Family conflicts between husband and wife are also fairly common in the Old Testament; I have already discussed one manifestation of such conflict in the various games that involved Adam and Eve (chapter 1) and Esther and Ahasuerus (chapter 7). The family, however, is not the only institutional setting in which conflict emerges between the sexes. Such conflict may also involve unmarried men and women, or third parties who disrupt the relationship between a husband and wife.

The provocation for a battle of the sexes may have little or nothing to do with differences between the sexes. Indeed, in two of the three conflicts analyzed in this chapter, the instigation of the conflict comes from outside the male-female relationship, in one case involving a demand for ⅃ reimbursement for services, in the other case an offer of money to extract some intelligence. Even the third conflict may have arisen for reasons other than incompatibility between the sexes, for it involved royal prerogatives as well.

The one thing the three conflicts I shall examine in this chapter share, besides the fact they all involve men and women at odds with each other, is an unmistakable attraction between the sexes. This attraction may be mutual, as it apparently was between David and Abigail, who succeeded in eliminating Abigail's husband, Nabal, in a triangular battle that pitted the lovers against the husband. But the love may be unrequited, as was Samson's for Delilah and Ahasuerus's for Vashti. Significantly, in the latter two battles of the sexes, it is the women who initiated the conflict and succeeded—at least temporarily—in getting their way.

But there is also justice for the men, though it is more long-term: Samson revenged his captors, and Ahasuerus, as I already showed (section 7.4), found a new and more pleasing wife in Esther after Vashti was banished. In the final section of this chapter, I shall assess implications of these outcomes for the rational play of games in which choices are conditioned by sexual bonds whose vicissitudes enmesh the characters.

8.2 A Love Triangle: Nabal, Abigail, and David

After Saul's reconciliation with David at the cave, David returned to the wilderness and initiated contact with a very wealthy man, whose shepherds he and his men had left unmolested:

The man's name was Nabal, and his wife's name was Abigail. The woman was intelligent and beautiful, but the man, a Calebite, was a hard man and an evildoer. (1 Sam. 25:3)

David dispatched ten young men to give his greetings to Nabal. But David also asked for something in return for protecting, or at least not interfering with, Nabal's shepherds:

Receive these young men graciously, for we have come on a festive occasion. Please give your servants and your son David whatever you can. (1 Sam. 25:8)

When Nabal balked at this request, David assembled four hundred of his men and prepared for battle. First, though, one of his men approached Abigail, condemning her "nasty" (1 Sam. 25:17) husband and saying that there would be ruination for his family. Horrified, Abigail, without informing Nabal, hastily put together presents for David, who had sworn not to leave Nabal "a single male of his" (1 Sam. 25:22) alive by morning.

When Abigail came upon David, she

quickly dismounted from the ass and threw herself face down before David, bowing to the ground. Prostrate at his feet, she pleaded, "Let the blame be mine, my lord, but let your handmaid speak to you; hear your maid's plea. Please, my lord, pay no attention to that wretched fellow Nabal. For he is just what his name says: His name means 'boor' and he is a boor." (1 Sam. 25:23–25)

Abigail gave David her presents and told him that because he was protected by God, bloodshed was unnecessary. David responded gratefully to Abigail's "prudence" (1 Sam. 25:33), and to God for sending her to him, by calling off his attack:

Praised be the LORD, the God of Israel, who sent you this day to meet me! And blessed be your prudence, and blessed be you yourself for restraining me from seeking redress in blood by my own hands. . . . Go up to your home safely. See, I have heeded your plea and respected your wish. (1 Sam. 25:32–35)

The next phase of the game commenced when Abigail confronted her husband with the truth of her appearance before David:

When Abigail came home to Nabal, he was having a feast in his house, a feast fit for a king; Nabal was in a merry mood and very drunk, so she did not tell him anything at all until daybreak. The next morning, when Nabal had slept off the wine, his wife told him everything that had happened; and his courage died within him, and he became like a stone. About ten days later the LORD struck Nabal and he died. (1 Sam. 25:36–38)

If this does not sound like divine intervention, consider the fairy-tale ending to this story:

David sent messengers to propose marriage to Abigail, to take her as his wife. (1 Sam. 25:39)

Not everyone, I venture to say, will be delighted by the manner in which Abigail accepted David's proposal:

She immediately bowed low with her face to the ground and said, "Your handmaid is ready to be your maidservant, to wash the feet of my lord's servants." (1 Sam. 25:41)

If one can skim off the more fantastic elements of this story, I believe there is a serious game lying below the surface. Abigail is without doubt an unhappy woman in her marriage. She abhors Nabal. So after hearing that David is out to avenge Nabal's insult to him, she never gives a second thought to taking matters into her own hands. Without Nabal's consent, she sets up David's first move—to accept her appeal or not—in the game tree shown in figure 8.1.

If David accepts Abigail's appeal, Abigail either can inform Nabal of her intercession before David or remain silent. While Abigail knows that David has already agreed to save her, her "nasty" (1 Sam. 25:17) husband remains a thorn in her side. By flaunting her success with David, and belittling Nabal's ineffectiveness against him, I assume Abigail hoped to induce his death.

Finally, after Nabal passed from the scene, David could choose whether or not to propose to the beautiful woman who so captivated him. After widowhood, such behavior was no longer unseemly, and neither was it unseemly for Abigail to accept David's proposal.

I believe David and Abigail's preferences for the four different outcomes shown in figure 8.1 were identical. They both most preferred marriage (4); if David did not propose, their prospects would be less certain, so I rate this outcome as next best (3). Worse could be Abigail's holding back on informing

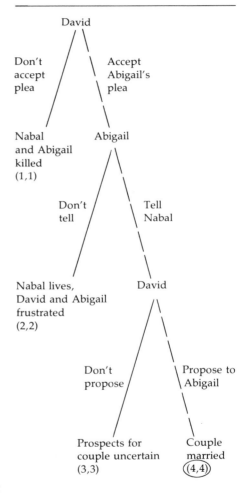

Key:
(x,y) = (David, Abigail)
4 = best; 3 = next best; 2 = next worst;
1 = worst
Circled outcome rational

Figure 8.1 Game tree of David and Abigail plot

Nabal of her infidelity to him (2); while Nabal would presumably be no worse for having been so deceived, this is good for neither David nor Abigail, who still have to deal with him.

I assume the worst outcome for David and Abigail would occur if David turned down Abigail's appeal at the start, for David would be guilt-stricken for taking "redress in blood" (1 Sam. 25:33), which could poison his future kingship. Abigail presumably would be killed along with Nabal for the arrogance of her husband, and David would of course not be able to marry the woman who so entranced him.

Working backward up the game tree in figure 8.1, it is easy to show that the rational outcome for both David and Abigail is to marry, which is also the best outcome (4) for both these players in this *game of total agreement* (as compared with games of total conflict and partial conflict, defined in sections 2.4 and 2.5). The choices that lead to this blissful if subservient state for Abigail involve her first turning David around from his plan to destroy Nabal and his family, then destroying Nabal herself.

The Bible does not specifically say that David was seduced by Abigail, but she seems not beyond such contrivance. That she held sway over David is clear from the following statement he made to her:

For as sure as the LORD, the God of Israel, lives—who has kept me from harming you—had you not come quickly to meet me, not a single male of Nabal's line would have been left by daybreak. (1 Sam. 25:34)

What finally won David over, I believe, was Abigail's skillful mixing of entreaty and flattery during their first encounter. Specifically, when Abigail told David that God "will fling away the lives of your enemies as from the hollow of a sling" (1 Sam. 25:29), it was logical for him to believe that the ingrate Nabal, whom Abigail had already labeled "nasty," would be so dispatched. (In this manner, David could thus surmise future moves in the game, which is the assumption underlying my designation of the rational choice shown in the game tree of figure 8.1.) It remained only for Abigail to deliver the mortifying blow to her husband's pride.

Although Abigail's beauty was certainly a factor in winning over David, she still felt compelled to make matters explicit, cleverly reminding David that his future prosperity and her own salvation were inextricably linked.

And when the LORD has prospered, my lord, remember your maid. (1 Sam. 25:31)

In sum, I believe Abigail's ravishing beauty and compelling logic finally melted David's resistance.

When the air was cleared by Nabal's demise, there was nothing to stand in the way of David and Abigail. I think it not unfair to characterize them as "plotters," because David and Abigail are nothing if not devious. Is not David's request to Nabal for a "protection" payment just a polite form of extortion? Nabal, despite his reputed bad character, was not reneging on any prior agreement.

As for Abigail, if she did not literally kill Nabal, then she did the next best thing by telling him something that made him out to be a weakling and a fool. Struck down by this realization, Nabal must have felt as if David and Abigail had actively conspired against him. Nabal, I believe, did have a point when he asked David's men in the beginning:

Should I then take my bread and my water, and the meat that I slaughtered for my own shearers, and give them to men who come from I don't know where? (1 Sam. 25:11)

Although Nabal may have been a drunkard and a bad husband, in my opinion he was treated shabbily when he refused to be cowed by a spiteful David and later fell prey to a scheming Abigail.

God never said anything Himself in the entire affair, but David sees His hand at work in the happy resolution of his problem with Nabal:

When David heard that Nabal was dead, he said, "Praised be the LORD who championed my cause against the insults of Nabal and held back His servant from wrongdoing; the LORD has brought Nabal's wrongdoing down on his own head." (1 Sam. 25:39)

I cannot say whether this adulation of God is deserved, but I would argue that the facts of the story are also consistent with the existence of a love triangle, in which it was rational for the two (would-be) lovers to dispatch the husband—independent of the part God might have played.

8.3 Samson's Revenge

Like the birth of Esau and Jacob (section 4.3), the birth of Samson is attended to by God, whose angel predicted:

He shall be the first to deliver Israel from the Philistines. (Judg. 13:5)

This miraculous birth occurred at the time when the Israelites were in their usual state of dissatisfaction, with the expected results:

The Israelites again did what was offensive to the LORD, and the LORD delivered them into the hands of the Philistines for forty years. (Judg. 13:1)

After Samson grew up, he quickly manifested carnal desires that were quite ecumenical:

Once Samson went down to Timnah; and while in Timnah, he noticed a girl among the Philistine women. On his return, he told his father and mother, "I noticed one of the Philistine women in Timnah; please get her for me as a wife." His father and mother said to him, "Is there no one among the daughters of your own kinsmen and among all our people, that you must go and take a wife from the uncircumcised Philistines?" (Judg. 14:1-3)

Samson also revealed himself to be rather surly with his father, though the Bible explains that God was surreptitiously manipulating events:

But Samson answered his father, "Get me that one, for she is the one that pleases me." His father and mother did not realize that this was the LORD's doing: He was seeking a pretext against the Philistines, for the Philistines were ruling over Israel at that time. (Judg. 14:3-4)

The woman indeed pleased Samson, and he took her as his wife. At a feast, Samson posed a riddle that stumped everybody, and the celebrants appealed to Samson's wife for help:

Coax your husband to provide us with the answer to the riddle; else we shall put you and your father's household to the fire; have you invited us here in order to impoverish us? (Judg. 14:15)

Samson's wife was distraught and accused her husband of not loving her, even hating her. At first Samson refused to tell his wife the answer to the riddle, but because she

continued to harass him with her tears, . . . on the seventh day he told her, because she nagged him so. (Judg. 14:17)

Angered by the whole business, Samson "left in a rage for his father's house" (Judg. 14:19). Ironically,

Samson's wife then married one of those who had been his wedding companions. (Judg. 14:20)

Samson then had second thoughts about abandoning his wife. When told by his wife's father that it was too late to reconsider, Samson flew into a rage and declared:

Now the Philistines can have no claim against me for the harm I shall do them. (Judg. 15:3)

After devastating their fields and vineyards, Samson fought a couple of vicious battles with them. Included among the victims in these cruel encounters were Samson's ex-wife and father-in-law, who were burned to death by the Philistines.

Samson came out of these battles with a reputation as a ferocious warrior of inhuman strength. This served him well as judge of Israel for twenty years. Samson also cemented his reputation as a man of the flesh by his encounters with prostitutes and other dalliances.

This background on Samson's early life, I believe, helps to make explicable his reckless behavior in his last and fatal tryst with a woman named Delilah. She was a Philistine with whom Samson fell in love.

Apparently, Samson's love for Delilah was not reciprocated. Rather, Delilah was more receptive to serving as bait for Samson for appropriate recompense. The lords of the Philistines made her a proposition:

Coax him and find out what makes him so strong, and how we can overpower him, tie him up, and make him helpless; and we'll each give you eleven hundred shekels of silver. (Judg. 16:5)

After assenting, Delilah asked Samson:

Tell me, what makes you so strong? And how could you be tied up and be made helpless? (Judg. 16:6)

Samson replied:

If I were to be tied with seven fresh tendons, that had not been dried, I should become as weak as an ordinary man. (Judg. 16:7)

After Delilah bound Samson as he had instructed her, she hid men in the inner room and cried, "Samson, the Philistines are upon you" (Judg. 16:9)! Samson's lie quickly became apparent:

Whereat he pulled the tendons apart, as a strand of tow [flax] comes apart at the touch of fire. So the secret of his strength remained unknown.

Then Delilah said to Samson, "Oh, you deceived me; you lied to me! Do tell me how you could be tied up." (Judg. 16:9-10)

Twice more Samson gave Delilah incorrect information about the source of his strength, and she became progressively more frustrated by his deception. In exasperation, Delilah exclaimed:

"How can you say you love me, when you don't confide in me? This makes three times that you've deceived me and haven't told me what makes you so strong." Finally, after she had nagged him and pressed him constantly, he was wearied to death and he confided everything to her. (Judg. 16:15–17)

The secret, of course, was Samson's long hair. When he told it to Delilah and she had it shaved off while Samson slept, the jig was up when he was awakened:

For he did not know that the LORD had departed from him. The Philistines seized him and gouged out his eyes. They brought him down to Gaza and shackled him in bronze fetters, and he became a mill slave in the prison. After his hair was cut off, it began to grow back. (Judg. 16:20–22)

Thus is a slow time bomb set ticking. Ineluctably, the climax approaches when Samson is summoned and made an object of derision and sport by the Philistines in a great celebration:

They put him between the pillars. And Samson said to the boy who was leading him by the hand, "Let go of me and let me feel the pillars that the temple rests upon, that I may lean on them." Now the temple was full of men and women; all the lords of the Philistines were there, and there were some three thousand men and

women on the roof watching Samson dance. Then Samson called to the LORD, "O Lord GOD! Please remember me, and give me strength just this once, O God, to take revenge of the Philistines if only for one of my two eyes." (Judg. 16:25–28)

Samson, his emasculated strength now restored, avenged his captors in an unprecedented biblical reprisal that sealed both his doom and the Philistines':

He embraced the two middle pillars that the temple rested upon, one with his right arm and one with his left, and leaned against them; Samson cried, "Let me die with the Philistines!" and he pulled with all his might. The temple came crashing down on the lords and on all the people in it. Those who were slain by him as he died outnumbered those who had been slain by him when he lived. (Judg. 16:29–30)

Like Esther and Mordecai's revenge on Haman (section 7.4), there is irony in this reversal of roles—the victim becomes the vanquisher. I would not suggest, however, that Samson, intrepid warrior that he was, planned for his own mutilation and ridicule only to provide himself with the later opportunity to retaliate massively against the Philistines. Perhaps this was in God's design, as hinted at by the angel at Samson's birth. The more explicit reference to God's "seeking a pretext against the Philistines" (Judg. 14:4) when Samson married reinforces this view.

To me, however, these auguries smack of insertions probably made for didactic purposes. They are not central to the narrative, which proceeds well enough without these lessons being drawn.

These didactic references present another problem: God's apparent meddling once again contradicts the free will man is presumed to have (section 2.3). Also, if God is playing some kind of undercover game, why should He want so much to help the Israelites after the Bible reports that He delivered them into the hands of the Philistines? In short, the signals given by references to God's purpose and control of affairs are confusing.

By comparison, I think Samson's behavior as both a truculent warrior and an insatiable lover is consistent and credible. On occasion, perhaps, Samson's strength strains credibility, as when he reportedly slays a thousand men with the jawbone of an ass. Other incidents in his life, such as tearing a lion to pieces, also are stupendous feats, but they are really no more than the normal hyperbole one finds in the Bible. Unquestionably, miraculous achievements, whether God-inspired or not, add drama to the stories, but

in my opinion a rational interpretation should not stand or fall on whether they can be explained in commonplace terms.

If Samson's immense strength, or its source, seem beyond human capabilities, his passion for women is not so hard to believe. As the story of his adult life demonstrates, Samson lusted after several women, and Delilah was not the first to whose blandishments he fell prey. When he gave in to his wife after she badgered him for several days, the pattern was set; he would not withhold information if the right woman was around to wheedle it out of him. While Samson could fight the Philistines like a fiend, he could readily be disarmed by women after whom he hankered.

The outcome matrix of the game Samson played with Delilah is shown in figure 8.2. Samson's desire having been kindled, Delilah could trade on it either by nagging Samson for the secret of his strength or not nagging him and hoping it would come out anyway. Samson, in turn, could either tell the secret of his strength or not tell it. Consider the outcomes for each pair of strategy choices:

Samson reluctant, Delilah persuasive (3,3): the next-best outcome for both players, because, though Delilah would prefer not to nag (if Samson tells) and Samson would

	Samson	
	Tell secret (T)	Don't tell secret (T̄)
Nag Samson (N)	Samson reluctant, Delilah persuasive (3,3)	Samson harassed, Delilah frustrated (1,1)
Don't nag Samson (N̄)	Samson forthcoming, Delilah happy (4,2)	Samson unforthcoming, Delilah unhappy (2,4)

Delilah

Key:
(x,y) = (Delilah, Samson)
4 = best; 3 = next best; 2 = next worst; 1 = worst

Figure 8.2 Outcome matrix of Samson's harassment

	Samson			
	T/T	T̄/T̄	T/T̄	T̄/T
N	(3,3)	(1,1)	((3,3))	(1,1)
N̄	(4,2)	(2,4)	(2,4)	(4,2)

Delilah

} Neither strategy dominant— must anticipate Samson's choice

↑
Tit-for-tat dominant

Key:
(x,y) = (Delilah, Samson)
4 = best; 3 = next best; 2 = next worst; 1 = worst
Circled outcome rational

Figure 8.3 Payoff matrix of Samson's harassment

prefer not to succumb (if Delilah doesn't nag), Delilah gets her way and Samson avoids further harassment.

Samson harassed, Delilah frustrated (1,1): the worst outcome for both players, because Samson does not get peace of mind, and Delilah is frustrated in her effort to learn Samson's secret.

Samson forthcoming, Delilah happy (4,2): the next-worst outcome for Samson, because he gives away his secret without good reason; the best outcome for Delilah, because she learns Samson's secret without making a pest of herself.

Samson unforthcoming, Delilah unhappy (2,4): the best outcome for Samson, because he keeps his secret and is not harassed; the next-worst outcome for Delilah, because Samson withholds his secret, though she is not frustrated in an attempt to obtain it.

I shall shortly consider a plausible reordering of Delilah's preferences.

The 2 × 4 payoff matrix of this harassment game is shown in figure 8.3, in which Delilah is assumed to have the first move and Samson is assumed to respond to her choice of a strategy. Anticipating Samson's choice of his dominant tit-for-tat strategy (T/T̄), Delilah would choose to nag Samson (N) since "3" is better for her than "2" in Samson's tit-for-tat column. This im-

plies Samson's choice of telling the secret of his strength, resulting in outcome (3,3), the next-best outcome for both players and that which actually occurred in the game.

In this game, I presume, Samson did not anticipate the consequence of having his eyes gouged out and being derided as a fool before the Philistines. On the other hand, since he was able later to wreak destruction on thousands of Philistines at the same time that he ended his own humiliation, it seems not unfair to characterize the denouement of this story as next best for Samson. Perhaps Samson foresaw that succumbing to Delilah would create problems, but he never anticipated his choice would result in vilification and torture and, ultimately, death.

Though he surrendered his secret to the treacherous Delilah, Samson apparently never won her love, which seems to be the thing he most wanted. In fact, Delilah's decisive argument in coaxing the truth out of Samson evidently was that because he did not confide in her, he did not love her. What better way was there for Samson to scotch this contention, and prove his love, than to comply with her request, even if it meant courting disaster?

As for Delilah's preferences, I think it hard to quarrel with the assumption that her two best outcomes were associated with Samson's telling his secret. I am less sure, however, about the order of preferences she held for her two worst outcomes. It seems to me, contrary to the representations given in figures 8.2 and 8.3, that Delilah might have preferred to nag Samson than not had he in the end repudiated her. For even though she would have failed to obtain Samson's secret, Delilah would perhaps have felt less badly after having tried than if she had made no effort at all.

If this is the case, then "2" and "1" for Delilah would be interchanged in the outcome and payoff matrices of figures 8.2 and 8.3. This switch, however, would make no difference in the rational outcome of (3,3) in the figure 8.3 payoff matrix: Samson's tit-for-tat strategy would remain dominant; Delilah now, however, anticipating Samson's choice, would prefer "3" to "1" (instead of "2"). Thus, the alternative assumption about Delilah's preferences would still render the actual choices of the players in this game, yielding outcome (3,3), rational.

Samson's incorrigible weakness for the women he loved sharply contrasts with his strength as a warrior and judge of Israel. In the final story of conflict between the sexes, this contrast is less sharply etched, though the love for a woman almost overrides the political judgment of a man.

8.4 The Cashiering of Queen Vashti

Before dispatching Haman (section 7.4), King Ahasuerus faced personal problems in his own household. In the third year of his reign, both he and his queen, Vashti, gave banquets for the men and women, respectively, of Shushan, the capital city.

On the seventh day of the banqueting, when the king was "merry with wine" (Esther 1:10), he ordered his seven eunuchs

to bring Queen Vashti before the king wearing a royal diadem, to display her beauty to the people and the officials; for she was a beautiful woman. But Queen Vashti refused to come at the king's command conveyed by the eunuchs. The king was greatly incensed, and his fury burned within him. (Esther 1:11–12)

But before doing anything rash, Ahasuerus consulted with his sages, who were versed in law and precedent. He asked them:

What shall be done, according to law, to Queen Vashti for failing to obey the command of King Ahasuerus conveyed by the eunuchs? (Esther 1:15)

One of the sages, Memucan, began with a shrewd calculation that touched hardly at all on Ahasu-erus's personal situation:

Queen Vashti has committed an of-fense not only against Your Majesty but also against all the officials and against all the peoples in all the prov-inces of King Ahasuerus. For the queen's behavior will make all wives despise their husbands, as they reflect that King Ahasuerus himself ordered Queen Vashti to be brought before him, but she would not come. This very day ladies of Persia and Media, who have heard of the queen's be-havior, will cite it to all Your Maj-esty's officials, and there will be no end of scorn and provocation! (Esther 1:16–18)

Following up on this prediction of a breakdown in the social order, Memucan recommended that a royal edict be issued that

Vashti shall never enter the presence of King Ahasuerus. And let Your Maj-esty bestow her royal state upon an-other who is more worthy than she. Then will the judgment executed by Your Majesty resound throughout your realm, vast though it is; and all wives will treat their husbands with respect, high and low alike. (Esther 1:19–20)

This advice pleased Ahasuerus, so the edict was issued.

After the king's anger abated, however,

he thought of Vashti and what she had done and what had been decreed against her. (Esther 2:1)

Then, just when the reader's expec-tation is raised that Ahasuerus's re-membrance of Vashti will lead to her recall, the Bible says that the king's attendants suggested that the search for a successor begin. (This search, of course, resulted in Es-ther's accession to the throne.) The king was pleased by this sugges-tion, and Vashti is never heard from again.

The outcome matrix of the game Vashti initiated by her refusal to comply with the king's order is de-picted in figure 8.4. Vashti may either obey or disobey Ahasuerus's order to appear before him, and he in turn may either depose or not depose her.

I believe my ordering of outcomes from best to worst for each player in figure 8.4 is uncontroversial, so I shall not go through a detailed jus-tification of all the rankings. In-stead, I shall try to indicate in more qualitative terms how I see this game, comparing only some of the outcomes for the players.

Although the Bible does not say so, I think it is reasonable to sup-pose that Vashti did not delight in

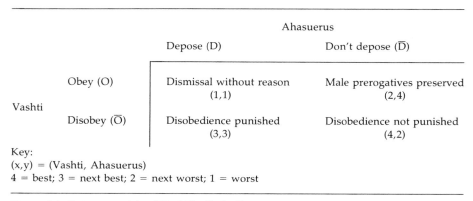

Key:
(x,y) = (Vashti, Ahasuerus)
4 = best; 3 = next best; 2 = next worst; 1 = worst

Figure 8.4 Outcome matrix of Vashti's disobedience

her role as queen. Subservient to a king she probably did not particularly like or respect, she therefore decided to rebel. Although this might seem an ill-advised act, I think that if Vashti thought that Ahasuerus truly loved her, he might cashier her as queen but not kill her. Accordingly, the worst outcome Vashti entertains by her defiance is "3"; while no longer queen, she would at least not be at Ahasuerus's beck and call, which I assume she bridles at because she herself is not in love with him.

On the other hand, should Ahasuerus be willing to forget, or paper over, her disobedience, Vashti would have established a healthy precedent which would better enable her to resist future encroachments on her freedom. Since she would still be queen, but now with

greater independence, I rate her successful defiance of Ahasuerus as her best outcome (4).

How does Ahasuerus see the game? Because he cares very much about Vashti, even after being spurned, he does not take lightly to dismissing her. That is why he consults with his sages after his anger has subsided. Of course, Ahasuerus would most prefer that Vashti obey him (4), but if she does not, he could better live with the situation in which she is deposed but alive (3) than that in which she remains as a defiant—and patently unloving—queen (2).

That Ahasuerus's ambivalence toward Vashti after her defiant act is deep-seated comes out particularly in the verse "he thought of Vashti" (Esther 2:1), quoted earlier in full. Translated, this verse means that Ahasuerus could not get Vashti off his mind, though by this time she was quite out of sight.

Ahasuerus is obviously saddened by his decision to depose Vashti. But he is genuinely persuaded, I believe, that the advice he received from Memucan was politically sound, and he is willing to stick by his decree.

The abrupt shift from the remembrance verse to the next verse describing the search for a new queen underscores the contradictory feelings within Ahasuerus—his attraction for Vashti and his political responsibility as king. By this time, though, the second motif dominates the first: it is time for Ahasuerus to shift gears in his life, and, therefore, the search for a successor should begin.

The payoff matrix in figure 8.5, to be sure, does not capture all these nuances. But it does say that Vashti, as the player with the first move, has a dominant strategy of disobeying, which does not require her to anticipate Ahasuerus's choice of his dominant tat-for-tit strategy. This results in outcome (3,3), the next-best outcome for both players and that which was actually realized in the game.

(Ahasuerus's tat-for-tit strategy might better be interpreted as "tit-for-tat," because it says Ahasuerus will not depose Vashti if she obeys; otherwise, he will depose her. The fact that "tit" is equated with "depose"—Ahasuerus's noncooperative strategy—is the reason for this switch in the usual meaning of tit-for-tat and tat-for-tit.)

The cashiering of Vashti, as previously shown (section 7.4), did not work out at all badly for Ahasuerus. He got a less brazen but equally beautiful queen who apparently loved him more than Vashti. Though I think Esther at a visceral level was just as tough as Vashti, she was certainly much softer and more discreet. It may malign women to say that they must be this way to be effective in a world of men, but this is one lesson that these two biblical stories seem to convey.

8.5 Conclusions

Conflict between the sexes has many guises, but in all cases I have considered it is fueled by the sexual attraction of at least one party for another. This is not to say that conflict between the sexes is impossible when the attraction is missing. But it is a different kind of conflict, the sort that, with the exception of the Adam and Eve story, has been the focus of analysis in all the preceding chapters.

In what way is conflict between sexually disinterested parties differ-

		Ahasuerus			
		D/D	$\overline{D}/\overline{D}$	D/$\overline{D}$	$\overline{D}$/D
Vashti	O	(1,1)	(2,4)	(1,1)	(2,4)
	$\overline{O}$	(3,3)	(4,2)	(4,2)	(3,3) ← Disobey dominant

↑
Tat-for-tit dominant

Key:
(x,y) = (Vashti, Ahasuerus)
4 = best; 3 = next best; 2 = next worst; 1 = worst
Circled outcome rational

Figure 8.5 Payoff matrix of Vashti's disobedience

ent in character from conflict in which sexual desire hangs heavy in the air? In my opinion, sexual desire creates a bond that makes it harder to evaluate one's position "objectively." The same, of course, can be said of the bond of family, but sexual attraction may be even stronger than blood ties.

This is why, I believe, Ahasuerus found it so difficult to let Vashti go. He pined for her after she was gone, but, for the sake of his kingdom, he knew he could make no other choice—lamentable as it was for him—than to banish her. Significantly, Ahasuerus did not kill Vashti, which I think she must have sensed would be the case when she made her bid for independence.

Samson also had a difficult time resisting Delilah—and his wife before her—when each exploited the love (lust?) he had for women. Once again the sexual bond proved hard to break, and Samson suffered greatly for succumbing to his carnal desires.

Abigail had no such problem with her reputedly nasty husband, Nabal, because the sexual attraction was not there. Indeed, she was quick to dump him after David appeared on the scene and evidently roused in her more desire (as well as fear). David reciprocated, and the bond that developed between them enabled Abigail guiltlessly to rid herself of Nabal, then establish a more satisfying conjugal relationship with David.

The conflicts studied here indicate different ways in which sex brings parties together or pulls them apart, depending on whom the sexual bond holds in thrall. In the main, unrequited love seems to be a destructive force, at least to the unloved. But I would maintain that the damage it causes may in fact redound to the ultimate advantage of most parties to a conflict. Abigail and David benefited at the expense of Nabal; Delilah got her silver; and Vashti, her freedom. Ahasuerus rebounded quite well from his personal grief, and even Samson got his revenge. Poor Nabal seems to have been the only true victim of sexual combat in the stories I have analyzed.

On the basis of these observations, I would conclude that while the sexual bond may complicate certain relationships, it in no way renders biblical characters irrational. They still seek to act in their self-interest, as the games analyzed demonstrate, but they are working within new constraints that sex adds to the mélange of emotions.

9

Theory, Evidence, and Findings

9.1 Evaluation of the Theory

In this section I shall evaluate the application of game theory and decision theory to the Old Testament, stressing particularly the advantages that a scientific theory brings to the analysis of the Bible. In section 9.2 I shall look more closely at the empirical evidence supporting the theory and summarize the main findings of the study. Finally, I shall conclude with more speculative remarks about God and the reasons for His behavior.

1. Weight of the evidence
To me the evidence is massive, detailed, and in the end overwhelming: games are played by biblical characters in the Old Testament. In story after story, positing biblical characters as players in games provides a natural interpretation of the events described.

2. Naturalness of the interpretation
To be sure, what I consider "natural" others may consider at best strained, at worst contrived. I am sympathetic to such criticism, but I would remind the critics who advance it that I do not pretend to capture every nuance in a payoff matrix or game tree; combing the Old Testament for fine shadings of meaning, characterization, and style was not what I set out to achieve. What I tried to do instead was delineate the central strategic

elements in a story, and to use game theory and decision theory to help me analyze them.

3. Focus on strategy

My focus on strategy, of course, depends critically on my reading of character motivations. While I have no theory for divining what motivates characters to act in particular ways, game theory obviously gives one a framework for putting words and actions together by its use of concepts like "strategy," "outcome," "payoff," and "rationality." The preceding chapters have shown, I believe, that these concepts are part and parcel of the thinking of biblical characters, even if they do not themselves articulate these concepts.

4. Elucidation of strategy

Strategies do not just pop into the heads of characters, who then tell the reader, in so many words, what exactly they plan to do. While characters are often clear about their preferences, the strategies they choose to try to implement them are often inchoate. Accordingly, the analyst, like a detective, must put the pieces together, relying on the insights of literary, psychological, and other approaches that might provide clues to the meaning of a passage, or its connection to other passages, in the Bible. I have not refrained from this detective work

but have engaged in it only insofar as I thought it would help me elucidate the plot and strategic calculations of characters in a story. Although I have not always been successful in culling a singular meaning out of every passage—and have said so—it has been surprising to me to find how much of the Old Testament is straightforward on the subject of strategy and the calculations underlying strategic choice. One does not have to do headstands to understand all the whys and wherefores, as some biblical scholars would have one believe. Sometimes there is *less* in a passage than meets the trained, but jaundiced, eye of the specialist, anxious to impute *some* meaning to it even when the evidence is flimsy.

5. Alternative interpretations

If there is a problem in reading the Old Testament for strategic content, it is less that it is obfuscatory than that nothing is said at all. When this is the case, it seems to me one has to admit *alternative* interpretations and assess their consequences, which I have done in several instances. To me this seems a better posture than to insist on *the* correct interpretation, however convoluted and unconvincing it is.

6. Discrimination using the theory

The power of game theory in biblical analysis lies not only in its ability to offer a point of view and organize information around it but also in its power to discriminate between better and worse alternative interpretations of character motivations. As I have shown in some of the ambiguous cases, not all motivational assumptions are consistent with what the Bible reports occurred. When this is true, the theory enables one to reject as inconsistent explanations based on these assumptions.

7. Scope of explanation

What constitutes "explanation" cannot be divorced from the fundamental postulates of the theory. Thus, explanations I have rejected, or interpretations I would not consider, might be acceptable to an analyst who thinks biblical characters do not play games, are not rational, and so forth. But, as I argued in (1) above, the preponderance of evidence as I read it is that biblical characters are game players and do act rationally, so I believe a refutation of this thesis must deal with the evidence I have presented, not just assert that the conception of "biblical games" is absurd. In other words, if the explanatory power of a game-theoretic interpretation of the Old Testament is to be rejected, it must be done so on the basis of the evidence—a story-by-story analysis demonstrating that biblical characters did not make, or could not have made, rational choices in the games studied.

8. Representativeness of the sample

It may be objected that this is asking too much—the theory may work well for some stories but not for others. Surely, this line of reasoning goes, since I have selected for analysis only those stories to which the theory is applicable, my sample is not representative. A proper test of the thesis that an underlying game-theoretic rationality is at work in the Old Testament requires an unbiased sample.

9. Disproof of the thesis

I readily admit to being selective in my choice of stories, but the question of bias is another matter. I looked for stories amenable to strategic analysis; I found many not to be and would make no claim about the rationality of individual choices in these. On the other hand, there certainly are stories in which strategic calculations loom large that I have not analyzed in the preceding chapters. However, most of these seem to me to be repetitious of the themes already discussed and hence do not contribute significant new insights, much less refute the thesis of this work.[1] So, while I cannot prove the lack of bias in my selection, I believe that the kind of game-theoretic rationality that so suffuses the stories analyzed here would not be lacking in other biblical stories in which strategic calculations are prominent.

10. Rigor and fruitfulness of the theory
If the scope and organizing power of game theory is broad, and its application to Old Testament stories is reasonably natural, the question remains whether it opens up vistas not perceptible without the intellectual clarification of the theory. I contend that it does, analytically by discriminating between motivational assumptions that work and do not work—as I indicated in (6) above—synthetically by providing a vocabulary and calculus that highlight common themes in different stories. This analytic-synthetic ability of the theory is a measure of its rigor and its fruitfulness (or heuristic value), though I would acknowledge that the theory is not the repository of all depth and subtlety that may grace this analysis. The theory also needs to be supplemented by an understanding of when its mindless application is inane. I am not sure I have avoided all inanity in the preceding chapters, but I hope those who find it will correct it with deeper insight and a more sophisticated understanding of biblical sources than I have. The Bible is not a brittle or sterile document, and neither should be its analysis.

11. Parsimony of the theory
A good theory should be not only self-correcting but also relatively simple and easy to apply. In my opinion, the game theory and decision theory used here so qualify, though it may not seem so to those with a fiercely humanistic bent. I can only say to those who find the formalism of payoff matrices and game trees unpalatable that my analysis will be embarrassingly unmathematical to game theorists, so I suspect I will not satisfy them, either. Yet I would maintain that this formalism, simple as it is, both summarizes a good deal in a story and highlights the central strategic choices of characters. The theory also provides a framework for assessing the rationality of these choices in a consistent way. The combination of economical description and simple logical structure gives the theory, as I have applied it, its parsimony. On occasion, to be sure, when I have embellished the stark, formal theory with more informal literary analysis, I have veered from the course of a rigorous theoretician hell-bent on scientific analysis. But the game theory/decision theory remain the common core and are what I believe bring overall coherence to the analysis.

9.2 Evaluation of the Evidence

1. Character of God
God is a study in contradictions: petty, manipulative, vindictive on the one hand, magnanimous, open, and forgiving on the other. One thing God never seems to be is modest or unassuming. When He

comes on stage, He is always front and center. His vanity seems boundless. Even when He remains in the wings, letting others speak for Him, His presence is dominating and magnetic, never aloof. As if He were incapable of harnessing His restless energy and being just a passive observer, God constantly meddles in human affairs, often upsetting previously harmonious relationships among people. (The monotony of peace and quiet may be one reason for God's intrusiveness, but I believe there are more fundamental strategic and psychological reasons that I shall explore further in this section and in section 9.3.) True, there are stories, like those described in the Book of Esther, in which God's name is never mentioned, but these are the exception. Moreover, even in these stories, there is certainly the strong hint of divine inspiration, as when the sages in Esther advise Ahasuerus (their wisdom must have some source), or when Ahasuerus cannot sleep and is reminded of Mordecai's life-saving service.

2. God as a game player

Unquestionably, God is a superlative strategist. Always suspicious and very touchy, He develops an obsession with testing the Israelites. Paradoxically, He seems secretly to hope they will not live up to His standards, thereby giving Him an opportunity to dramatize His own strength and their weakness. If this is His hope, it is amply fulfilled. But, though the Israelites continually fail Him, God never abandons them for good. Instead, He does what seems to come naturally: fulminates, punishes them, reneges, and then repeats the cycle when He uncovers new transgressions that rekindle His ire.

3. Assessment of God's retribution policy

Because it always has to be repeated, God's retribution policy must be judged only partially successful. But is there a better policy He could have adopted? If God had wiped out the Israelites for their idolatrous practices at Mount Sinai, instead of bowing to the pleas of Moses, it is doubtful that His problems would have been solved. After all, God almost destroyed the world when earlier He set Noah and the animals adrift in an ark (which is a story that could probably best be modeled as a one-person game, with God as the player), and what good did it do Him? After resigning Himself to the fact that He could not once and for all purge the human race of its recalcitrant members, God did the next best thing and tried to keep the miscreants in line through a policy of excoriation and unremitting punishment, especially when they included His chosen people.

4. Side benefit of retribution policy

This policy certainly had the side benefit of relieving any boredom God might have felt in a more placid world. If there had been no sinning by the people, God would not have had the opportunities He did to interfere in their affairs and thereby display His mighty power against the sinners. Thus, a policy of retribution works superbly for God: it keeps the people partially in check and induces them to be generally reverential, but it does not squelch all rebelliousness. Most disturbing, perhaps, are the cases in which God Himself stirs up trouble or even incites rebellion, only promptly to clamp down on it. Justice would not appear to be well served by such provocative behavior.

5. Is God just?

The question really is: Are God's goals, and the actions He takes to implement them as a game player, compatible with achieving human justice in the world? Insofar as what God regards as sinful is deemed nefarious behavior by society, the punishment God inflicts on sinners would seem to comport with what the populace considers just. But the populace does not always agree with God, or speak with one voice, in which case God usually takes sides.

6. Evidence of arbitrariness

An inescapable conclusion emerges from a comparative analysis of the stories I have discussed: God is not impartial. He favors some characters, scorns others. David, for example, is one of His favorites; he can do practically no wrong, despite a well-developed appetite for adultery. Saul, David's predecessor as king, is treated shabbily, presumably because God felt rejected when He deferred to the people and anointed Saul king. But God also expresses His displeasure for little apparent reason, as when he accepted Abel's offering but rejected Cain's, provoking in Cain incontinent jealousy that led to fratricide.

7. Character of man

A jealous Cain, a temptable Eve, a resolute Abraham, a grim Jephthah, a prevaricating Jacob, a wary Joseph, a vacillating and then forceful Moses, an obdurate Pharaoh, a gullible Joshua, a conspiratorial Rahab, a wise Solomon, an insecure Saul, a vengeful Samuel, a brazen Vashti, a shrewd Esther, a tactless Mordecai, a seductive Abigail, a carnal David, a lustful Samson, a venal Delilah—the gamut of personalities parades through the Old Testament. The greatest heroes of the Old Testament—men like Abraham, Moses, and David—are so in part because they are promoted and protected by God, though He is not above petulance in dealing with them. That He, for example, denied Moses entry into the promised land while granting him an unprecedented face-to-face meeting seems peevish to me.

8. Man's relationship to God

The personality of a character in part determines his preferences for outcomes, including those God may have had a hand in effecting. Whether or not a character's preferences coincide with God's, their *relationship* is defined by the game they play. Thus, I would submit that the central concern of theology—the relationship of man to God—can be given concrete expression in the games man plays with his Creator.

9. Faith in the relationship

Faith in God implies a special kind of coincidence in preference—man unquestionably accepts God's point of view, and wants to do so. A faithful man has a dominant, or unconditionally best, strategy of following God's precepts. But, as I have shown, even great figures like Abraham, while appearing to show their untrammeled faith by doing what God asked, may not have acted simply out of blind faith. They may have made a more sophisticated, game-theoretic calculation: anticipating God's preference, they

calculated that obedience to God's word would yield them a greater payoff than disobedience. Indeed, when the Bible is not explicit about a character's faith, there may be no way to distinguish a sophisticated show of faith from an unquestioning blind faith, which, moreover, may itself be fear-induced.

10. Human relationships

Human relationships are defined by games having exclusively human players, though God often stands as a towering figure in the background whose preferences condition the choices of the human players. The Gibeonites, for example, recalled God's destruction of Pharaoh's army when they attempted to negotiate a treaty with Joshua; Rahab also remembered the Egyptians' fate when she elected to conspire with the Israelite spies. While these players were ostensibly involved in games against human adversaries, they fully understood that God was not an indifferent observer.

11. Treachery in human relationships and its consequences

It is hard to find games with exclusively human players in the Old Testament in which at least one player is not acting treacherously toward another: Jacob deceives Esau; Joseph tricks his brothers; Pharaoh repeatedly retracts his promise; Rahab lies to her king; the Gibeonites lie to Joshua; Delilah hides her true intentions; Solomon covers up the import of his "solution." What is interesting is that both favored and unfavored characters—by God's lights—engage in what may charitably be described as less than forthcoming behavior, less charitably as chicanery and deceit. Nobody is excluded—even Abraham had a streak of mendacity in him as a young man. On the other hand, honesty, like Vashti's, is not always rewarded, though she is not executed for her forthrightness. Clearly, "good behavior" is not necessarily extolled, nor "bad behavior" condemned, in the Bible.

12. God's treachery

It is God's treachery that is most disturbing to observe. His cavalier treatment of Cain before he murdered Abel, His nearly interminable punishment of Pharaoh—whom He Himself made to act despicably—and His torpedoing of Saul after supporting him for the kingship are only the most glaring examples of what I consider God's callousness. To be sure, there are reasons for God's personal vendettas, as I have already shown, but that does not make His behavior above reproach by the normal canons of ethics. It only makes Him rational; rational actions may, speaking normatively, be thoroughly reprehensible.

9.3 Concluding Remarks on God

There is, of course, another side to God. He repeatedly helps the Israelites when they are oppressed or in distress, balking only when their demands become incessant or outrageous. He rewards Abraham, Isaac, and Jacob for their good deeds, and He bestows on Moses a reward second to none, after helping him at practically every step from his birth onward. Even some biblical characters whose behavior God finds repugnant, like Adam, Eve, Cain, and Jephthah, He allows to live out their full lives.

Yet, God's dark, melancholic side cannot be lightly dismissed. He intrudes in people's lives with unerring regularity, wrecking amicable relationships, punishing future generations for sins of the past, offering and then withdrawing His support. In my opinion, this inimical behavior stems principally from His overweening concern for His reputation.

God continually broods about it. He worries endlessly about how to enhance it. He is not so much concerned with the world as how He thinks the world sees Him. He is other-directed with a vengeance.

This, incidentally, is an eminently game-theoretic point of view: by trying to anticipate the behavior of others, one can better fashion one's own. But God's predictions are imperfect, because man, most of the time, is allowed free will. Lacking total control over situations, God must remain flexible and try to adapt to changing circumstances.

Manifestations of God's flexibility crop up frequently in the Old Testament. For example, God often decides on the spot whether to help or hurt the Israelites. He is also quite willing to change His mind when the exigencies of a situation demand it. After hearing Moses's appeal on behalf of the Israelites, for example, God reverses His initial judgment to annihilate them for their idolatry.

Heroes like Moses are not the only figures with influence. Even as refractory a figure as Cain is able to extract from God a pledge to spare his life, perhaps, as I suggested earlier, because God felt partially responsible for Cain's heinous crime.

God also exhibits notable flexibility in countermanding His order to Abraham to sacrifice Isaac. Of course, if testing Abraham were God's intention from the start, then His flexibility is also strategic in His rational choice of tit-for-tat. That is, this strategy does not indicate that God made a last-minute switch because He was flexible but rather that He tuned His response to Abraham's, a sort of premeditated flexibility He was unwilling to apply to Jephthah. Generally speaking, one cannot say unqualifiedly how far

into the future biblical characters—including God—plan their moves, but God, in my view, shows Himself to be rather open to persuasion and adaptable to others' responses. He is not capricious.

God's adaptiveness might be interpreted as a healthy open-mindedness. I do not dispute this view, but I would maintain that God's reason for acting this way is His inveterate other-directedness and self-consciousness. Because He is extremely sensitive about His image, it is rational for Him to rely on feedback, and be ready to change His mind when His soundings indicate that He will run into problems steering an inexorable course. This is the reason why, for example, after hearing rumblings for a king from the Israelites, God reluctantly gave them Saul.

With a flexible game player like God, it is not surprising that an immutable pattern in His behavior is hard to discern. Having to adapt to changing situations, it may, as I have argued, be rational for Him to support and then abandon figures like Adam, Jephthah, and Saul. Similarly, rationality may dictate coming to the aid of figures like Abraham, Moses, David, and Samson, though not necessarily easing all their travails or granting them all the recompense they think they deserve.

Like any good game player modulating His choices and responses, God is tentative about His judgments, conditional in His support. So are human players, like Joseph with his brothers, Moses with the Israelites, the spies with Rahab, and David with Saul. Indeed, as I argued earlier, a just agreement of the kind Rahab negotiated with the Israelite spies depends on the ability of the players to hold their counterparts to the agreement by repudiating it if a commitment is not forthcoming from the other side.

But God is not just another game player who can be lumped together with all the other biblical characters. He has not only special powers and grandiose ambitions but also a continuing presence. As a consequence of His immortality, God's actions have both an immediate effect and a resonant effect on future generations. Knowing this, He must choreograph His moves with an eye toward the image they will convey to potential players, perhaps not yet born, in games that are hard even to envision. Put another way, God is always playing in more than one game, but the parameters of the future games are not self-evident. God, as I stressed earlier, is neither omniscient nor omnipotent; He must therefore think carefully about the consequences of His choices and those of other players, both present and future.

This explains, I believe, why God is so concerned about His image. He as much wants to impress future adversaries—and those of us who read of His exploits in the Bible—as be a rational player in the here and now. God quite candidly confesses this motive on several occasions, citing on the one hand His beneficent treatment of Abraham, Isaac, and Jacob, and on the other His harsh treatment of Pharaoh. The good prosper, the bad succumb.

On balance, I think, God fosters a more negative than positive image in the Old Testament. He is fundamentally distrusting—His wrath is always close to the surface. When it breaks through—as it often does—it is sometimes for seemingly slight offenses, even offenses that He may have had a hand in fabricating.

The reason God leans toward the harsh side, I believe, is that, as a neophyte in the business of creating worlds—at least no previous experience is mentioned in the Bible—He wants to establish His credibility quickly. This is not so important in the immediate context as in the future games He will play or influence.

Right from the start, therefore, God punishes all His adversaries—Adam, Eve, and the serpent—with a vehemence. The murder of Abel, which God instigates, follows soon thereafter. The stigma that Cain is forced to bear for this sin is designed not just to teach him a lesson but also to serve as a deterrent to all the people whom the peripatetic Cain encounters, or who later hear about his punishment.

Besides the case of Cain, I have given other examples of mischief God fomented and then exploited to bolster His reputation for toughness. Yet I think God is probably not "innately" meddlesome or unreasonably harsh or vindictive. Rather, He is a constant worrier who believes He must cement His image as a vigorous disciplinarian. This, He thinks, will forestall later deviations, and indeed it does make some people like Rahab and the Gibeonites more God-fearing. It also induces them to be deceitful, which suggests that even God's most punitive actions do not necessarily expunge evil from the world.

God's anxiety about being perceived as weak or indecisive, in my view, is the explanation for His harshness—especially in the beginning—and for His extreme image-consciousness. But God does not want to appear to be just ruthless and cruel; like all of us, He wants also to be loved. Thus, He becomes despondent when He is rejected, jealous when other gods are worshiped. It is precisely these rather common failings—emotional problems, if you will—that, in my opinion, reflect the human, if humorless, side of God.

But is God human or, if not, the product of human imagination? I cannot say, but I believe the hypothesis that God is a figment is not untenable: He mirrors remarkably well the conflicts, the insecurity, in all of us, which makes it not impossible that the writers of the Bible were projecting their own hopes and fears—that is, a sentient conception of themselves writ large.[2] Plausible as this hypothesis is, I am unwilling to assert unequivocally that God is unreal and does not exist, except as a figment. There is not incontrovertible evidence that I know of—scientific or otherwise—that establishes that God does not, or could not, exist. While I have treated Him as a real player in this book, I hold in abeyance a judgment about His physical or spiritual form and psychological origins.

In a way, the Bible plays a game on us by implanting in our minds uncertainty about God's existence, form, and origins. While His reality seems at odds with contemporary, everyday experience for many people—myself included—His limpid presence is hard to dismiss. Could God be a chimera? Could the human imagination alone create God without the experiences reported in the Bible—rich and profound as they are—having a basis in reality? This tension between fiction and fact is what makes the Bible continually interesting; the deep questions it raises are never likely to be resolved. If there were a resolution, these questions would no longer be deep, and abiding interest in them would cease.

The Bible presents us with a kind of game, but it is one that has no solution. It terminates for us when we die, but this is a physical fact, not a solution. Religions offer spiritual solutions, but they are not intellectually satisfying to many people. Hence the search for understanding, a reconciliation of the natural and supernatural, continues. If the magic key—the theory to effect this reconciliation—were found, the tension between the natural and supernatural would be relieved, and the Bible would lose its mystery for us.

Game theory does *not* provide the magic key; the mystery remains impenetrable. But game theory does force one to come to grips with biblical characters and their dilemmas in a concrete setting—the games they play—placing at least some of the supernatural in a natural context. Moreover, it provides a theory to explain the behavior of God and His protagonists that is coherent, parsimonious, and rigorous.

In order to paint a more rounded picture of different kinds of conflicts in the Bible, I have supplemented the game-theoretic analysis with a psychological analysis of character motives, especially God's. Admittedly, the psychological analysis I have engaged in requires making certain inferential leaps from the text and is, therefore, more speculative than the game-theoretic analysis. Yet, by providing insight into the *origins* of the preferences posited in the game-theoretic analysis, it helps to show *why* characters tried to pursue the goals they did.

Given these goals—noble or base, material or spiritual—I think the evidence establishes that biblical characters are eminently rational in their pursuit of them. So is God, whose goals seem no less selfish or unselfish than those of other characters. The games they play are the stuff of biblical stories, but the fascination of the Bible lies not just in the strategic aspects of the games but also in what edification the games provide about God and His relationship to man.

As I have tried to show, God's personality is not inscrutable, nor is His game playing bizarre. Whether His personality traits and behavior make Him a transcendent Supreme Being or simply a larger-than-life human being—or figment—is hard to say. The enigma of God remains, even if His motives are clearer, His actions more understandable, and His character more palpable.

Notes

Chapter 1

1

John von Neumann and Oskar Morgenstern, *Theory of Games and Economic Behavior* (Princeton, N.J.: Princeton University Press, 1944).

2

In fact, the only serious attempt at literary analysis using game (and metagame) theory I know of is that by Nigel Howard of Harold Pinter's play, *The Caretaker*. See Nigel Howard, *Paradoxes of Rationality: Theory of Metagames and Political Behavior* (Cambridge, Mass.: MIT Press, 1971), pp. 140–146.

3

That strategic calculation is not absent from the New Testament is argued in Jay Haley, *The Power Tactics of Jesus Christ and Other Essays* (New York: Avon Books, 1971), pp. 29–68. Though Haley makes no use of formal game theory, his analysis of Jesus's career points up the rationality of some of his key decisions. In a similar vein, see Hugh J. Schonfield, *The Passover Plot: New Light on the History of Jesus* (New York: Bantam Books, 1967); and, more generally, Michael Grant, *Jesus: An Historian's View of the Gospels* (New York: Charles Scribner's Sons, 1977).

4

So, in a very different context, are probability theory and statistics, though these tools help answer very different questions. For a useful examination of the Old Testament, and rabbinic commentaries, in light of this branch of mathematics, see Nachum L. Rabinovitch, *Probability and Statistical Inference in Ancient and Medieval Jewish Literature*

(Toronto: University of Toronto Press, 1973).

5

Erich Auerbach, *Mimesis: The Representation of Reality in Western Literature*, tr. Willard R. Trask (Princeton, N.J.: Princeton University Press, 1953), chap. 1.

6

Ibid., p. 14.

7

Ibid., p. 22.

8

The Torah: The Five Books of Moses (2d ed., 1967); *The Five Megilloth and Jonah* (2d rev. ed., 1974); *The Prophets* (1978). For "a systematic account of the labors and reasoning of the committee that translated *The Torah*," see Harry M. Orlinsky (ed.), *Notes on the New Translation of the Torah* (Philadelphia: Jewish Publication Society of America, 1969). I am grateful to the Jewish Publication Society of America for permission to quote from their translations; the quotations are copyrighted by the Society and used through their courtesy. On the question of the best translation, and its importance to this work, I would echo the sentiment of Edmund Leach: "Since every word, indeed every letter of the Hebrew text has provided occasion for scholarly dispute I cannot pretend to one hundred percent accuracy but I do not think that this deficiency is of great significance. Only once or twice does my argument hang upon a point of linguistic detail. For the most part I am concerned with stories, not with texts" (*Genesis as Myth and Other Essays* [London: Jonathan Cape, 1969], p. 32).

Chapter 2

1

As expressed in a contemporary novel, God's view of the world He created is not so happy: "And God beheld what He had done and was saddened by His enthusiasm. I am not satisfied with what I am, He thought, and in my inventiveness and delight, I thought to make them like me, that seeing me within themselves they would wish for my company. And I, bored by my own entrancement, would be fulfilled by theirs. What mistake. Yes. Mistake." (Arthur A. Cohen, *In the Days of Simon Stern* [New York: Random House, 1972], p. 456). I thank William Scott Green for this reference.

2

Leszek Kolakowski, *The Key to Heaven*, tr. Celina Wieniewska and Salvator Attanasio (New York: Grove Press, 1972), p. 3.

3

Elie Wiesel, *Messengers of God: Biblical Portraits and Legends* (New York: Pocket Books, 1977), p. 104. Gordon D. Kaufman offers a developmental explanation for God's endowment of free will to man: "If God was trying to create free and responsible men, it was necessary that he give them scope within which to exercise their freedom and thus learn to become responsible" (*God the Problem* [Cambridge, Mass.: Harvard University Press, 1972], p. 191).

4

It is easy to show that the expansion of every 2 × 2 ordinal game in which preferences are strict (i.e., whose four outcomes can be ranked from best to worst without ties) to a 2 × 4 ordinal game always results in the second-moving player's having a dominant strategy, whether he had one or not in the 2 × 2 game. The rationality of choosing dominant strategies has been recently challenged by "Newcomb's problem," which has theological overtones and whose game-theoretic structure I analyze in "Newcomb's Problem and Prisoners' Dilemma," *Journal of Conflict Resolution* 19, no. 4 (December 1975): 596–612. The choice of dominant strategies is most questionable, in my opinion, in games in which there is a "paradox of inducement," but this paradox does not arise in any games discussed in this chapter. (See, however, section 3.3.) This paradox is elucidated in Steven J. Brams, *Paradoxes in Politics: An Introduction to The Nonobvious in Political Science* (New York: Free Press, 1976), chap. 5, and Nigel Howard, *Paradoxes of Rationality: Theory of Metagames and Political Behavior* (Cambridge, Mass.: MIT Press, 1971), pp. 168–184.

5

Encyclopedia of Biblical Interpretation (New York: American Biblical Encyclopedia Society, 1953), 1: 119; and John L. McKenzie, *Dictionary of the Bible* (Milwaukee: Bruce Publishing Company, 1965), p. 791. For more on the sexual role of serpents in mythology, see Robert Graves and Raphael Patai, *Hebrew Myths: The Book of Genesis* (New York: McGraw-Hill, 1963), pp. 86–87. Philological analysis that goes well beyond a literal interpretation of the biblical text I prefer not to rely on too heavily. Nevertheless, biblical interpretations that range from rabbinic to Freudian should, I believe, not be precluded out

of hand. What the text makes plain is most defensible, but this view should not make one so literal-minded as to depreciate good insights that other scholarship may yield. I hope, incidentally, that such a catholic perspective on biblical interpretation is applied to this book!

6

On the other hand, it may be argued that, whatever the circumstances, God most wanted an excuse for punishing Adam and Eve. Thereby He could then set an eye-opening precedent for what befalls those who try to defy His prohibitions. This view is consistent with God's most wanting Adam and Eve to succumb to temptation in the games that they played with the serpent and each other. I shall return to this argument for establishing precedents—and future credibility—repeatedly throughout this book.

7

From another passage in the Bible (Ezek. 28:11–19), however, it appears that God was less upset by the moral knowledge Adam and Eve gained from eating the forbidden fruit than from the hubris they displayed in daring to defy Him.

8

See Frederic Schick, "Some Notes on Thinking Ahead," *Social Research* 44, no. 3 (Autumn 1977):786–800.

Chapter 3

1

For an alternative motive that emphasizes Abraham's desire to protect his wife rather than himself, see *The Anchor Bible: Genesis*, introduction, translation and notes by E. A. Speiser (Garden City, N.Y.: Doubleday & Company, 1964), pp. XL–XLI. Whatever Abraham's precise motive, he appears not to have been above calculation.

2

For a description of Prisoners' Dilemma and examples of its occurrence in politics, see Steven J. Brams, *Paradoxes in Politics: An Introduction to the Nonobvious in Political Science* (New York: Free Press, 1976), chaps. 4 and 8; and Steven J. Brams, *Game Theory and Politics* (New York: Free Press, 1975) chaps. 1 and 4. In fact, interpretations (a) and (b), as well as interpretations (a), (b), and (c) of the vindictive interpretation of God's preferences (to be discussed), exhibit another kind of paradox: the player with the dominant strategy (God) does worse than the player without one (Jephthah). This paradox is discussed in *Paradoxes in Politics*, chap. 5, and is called the "inducement paradox." It was discovered in the so-called White House tapes game, played between President Nixon and Supreme Court justices Burger and Blackman in 1974, just before Nixon resigned in the wake of Watergate. See Steven J. Brams, *The Presidential Election Game* (New Haven: Yale University Press, 1978), chap. 5.

3

Søren Kierkegaard, *Fear and Trembling*, tr. Walter Lowrie (Princeton, N.J.: Princeton University Press, 1954).

4

Leszek Kolakowski, *The Key to Heaven*, tr. Celina Wieniewska and Salvator Attanasio (New York: Grove Press, 1972), p. 18.

5

Ibid., p. 19. Franz Kafka also pokes fun at Abraham's character, saying he "was prepared to satisfy the demand for a sacrifice immediately, with the promptness of a waiter, but was unable to bring it off because he could not get away, being indispensable . . . this the Bible also realized, for it says: 'He set his house in order'" (*Parables and Paradoxes* [New York: Schocken Books, 1958], p. 41).

6

Kierkegaard, *Fear and Trembling*, p. 27.

7

Rashi: Commentaries on the Pentateuch, tr. Chaim Pearl (New York: W. W. Norton & Co., 1970), pp. 51–52. Isaac is, in fact, slain by Abraham in the antiwar poem by Wilfred Owen, "The Parable of the Old Man and the Young," in which the old man also slew "half the seed of Europe, one by one." See *The Collected Poems of Wilfred Owen*, ed. C. Day Lewis (Norfolk, Conn.: New Directions Books, 1964), p. 42. For a detailed analysis of sources, and interpretation of commentary, on Abraham's sacrifice as rendered in a twelfth-century poem, "Akedah," by a certain Rabbi Ephraim of Bonn, see Shalom Spiegel, *The Last Trial*, tr. Judah Goldin (New York: Pantheon Books, 1967).

8

Their dominant strategies, of course, may indicate *fear* of God as much as faith, but the Bible provides insufficient information to say whether Abraham and Jephthah's possible blind faith was fear-induced. The element of fear is, however, expressed in the lyrics of Bob Dylan's song, "Highway 61 Revisited":

Oh God said to Abraham, "Kill me a son"
Abe says, "Man, you must be puttin' me on"
God say, "No." Abe say, "What?"
God say, "You can do what you want, Abe, but
The next time you see me comin' you better run,"
Well, Abe says, "Where do you want this killin' done?"

© 1965 Warner Bros. Inc. All Rights Reserved. Used By Permission. I thank Jeffrey T. Richelson for this reference.

9

"Jephthah," in *Encyclopedia Judaica* (Jerusalem: Keter Publishing House, 1971), 9: 1342.

10

Differences between biblical narratives and Greek mythology, as exemplified in the writings of Homer, are discussed in Eric Auerbach, *Mimesis: The Representation of Reality in Western Literature,* tr. Willard R. Trask (Princeton, N.J.: Princeton University Press, 1953), chap. 1.

Chapter 4

1

A contrary view that Abel's murder was unpremeditated is taken in Nahum M. Sarna, *Understanding Genesis: The Heritage of Biblical Israel* (New York: Schocken Books, 1970), p. 31.

2

It might also be read as a challenge to God's omniscience—and His complicity—as suggested by the natural follow-up question: "Why should One who watches over all creatures ask one, unless He planned the murder Himself?"

See Robert Graves and Raphael Patai, *Hebrew Myths: The Book of Genesis* (New York: McGraw-Hill Book Company, 1963), p. 92. God's role as an accomplice in the murder is also considered, though rejected, by Elie Wiesel: "Cain could not help but kill: he did not choose the crime; instead the crime chose him" (*Messengers of God: Biblical Portraits and Legends* [New York: Pocket Books, 1977], p. 58). I find this line of argument, which says that Cain effectively did not make a choice but was preconditioned to respond, unpersuasive. Cain's response, as I argued earlier, was not an emotional outburst but instead was apparently planned. If this is so, it follows that Cain could anticipate being discovered by God and plan for his defense.

3

Alternatively, one might argue that Abel's blood did not so much elicit shame and self-blame in God as impel Him to avenge Cain's crime. But this interpretation would not explain why God did not respond in kind and simply kill Cain. (See subsequent text.)

Chapter 5

1

James S. Ackerman, "The Literary Context of the Moses Birth Story (Exodus 1–2)," in *Literary Interpretations of Biblical Narratives,* ed. Kenneth R. R. Gros Louis, James S. Ackerman, and Thayer S. Warshaw (Nashville, Tenn.: Abingdon Press, 1974), p. 85.

2

This interpretation, however, is contradicted by an earlier statement God made to Moses: "But," He said, "you cannot see My face, for man may not see Me and live" (Exod. 33:20).

3

This duality in Moses's character has long been recognized but, in my opinion, never satisfactorily explained. For some psychological speculations, see David Daiches, *Moses: The Man and His Vision* (New York: Praeger, 1975), p. 151. On the psychoanalytic origins of monotheism, as enunciated in the Mosaic code, see Sigmund Freud, *Moses and Monotheism* (New York: Vintage, 1939); Freud's work is dismissed as "unscientific" and "based on groundless hypotheses" in Martin Buber, *Moses: The Revelation and the Covenant* (New York: Harper and Row, 1958), p. 7.

Chapter 6

1

Since Joshua, the Gibeonites believed, had through Moses been promised "the whole land," and all inhabitants had been slated to be "wipe[d] out" (Josh. 9:24), it must have seemed very likely to them that they would be unmasked at some point. Then, and only then, would having a treaty save them.

2

Sissela Bok, *Lying: Moral Choice in Public and Private Life* (New York: Pantheon Books, 1978), offers a good analysis of such questions. See also Steven J. Brams, "Deception in 2 × 2 Games," *Journal of Peace Science,* 2(Spring 1977): 171–203; and Steven J. Brams and Frank C. Zagare, "Deception in Simple Voting Games," *Social Science Research,* 6(September 1977): 257–272.

Chapter 9

1

To take two examples, David's triangular relationship with Bathsheba and Uriah in the Second Book of Samuel reflects some of the same romantic and strategic cross-currents as the David-Abigail-Nabal triangle analyzed in section 8.2; the meaning of faith that is expostulated in the Book of Job is essentially the same as that derived from the two stories of sacrifice in chapter 3, though Job's monumental and extended suffering add great poignancy to his story.

2

For a fascinating argument that the gods of ancient times—and presumably God later—were not figments but rather *"were* man's volition . . . occupied his nervous system, probably his right hemisphere, and from stores of admonitory and preceptive experience, transmuted this experience into articulated speech which then 'told' man what to do," see Julian Jaynes, *The Origin of Consciousness in the Breakdown of the Bicameral Mind* (Boston: Houghton Mifflin, 1976), pp. 202–203; italics in original. On the wildly different precepts early Christians heard—or found politically expedient to hear—see Elaine Pagels, *The Gnostic Gospels* (New York: Random House, 1979).

General Index

Index of Biblical Passages